THE MOMENT THE LITTLE BOY SAW
THE LAMA, HE WENT TO HIM . . .

The Lama Kewtsang Rinpoché of Sera Monastery was disguised in a cloak, but round his neck he was wearing a rosary which had belonged to the Thirteenth Dalai Lama. The little boy seemed to recognize the rosary, and he asked to be given it. The lama promised to give it to him if he could guess who he was, and the boy replied that he was Sera-aga, which meant, in the local dialect, "a lama of Sera." The lama asked who the "master" was, and the boy gave the name of Losang. He also knew the name of the real servant, which was Amdo Kasang.

The lama spent the whole day watching the little boy with increasing interest, until it was time for the boy to be put to bed. All the party stayed in the house for the night, and early the next morning, when they were making ready to leave, the boy got out of his bed and insisted that he wanted to go with them.

I was that boy.

"Earnestness, greatness of heart, simplicity of soul shine from these pages."
                                                    —*Kirkus Reviews*

An Alternate Selection of One Spirit™
and of Book-of-the-Month Club®

Selected Works by
His Holiness the Dalai Lama

*Healing Anger: The Power of Patience
from a Buddhist Perspective*

*The Good Heart: A Buddhist Persective on
the Teachings of Jesus*

The Path to Enlightenment

*The Global Community and the Need
for Universal Responsibility*

Compassion and the Individual

Path to Bliss

The Meaning of Life

Policy of Kindness

Freedom in Exile

The Union of Bliss and Emptiness

Transcendent Wisdom

The Buddhism of Tibet

Deity Yoga in Action and Performance Tantras

Tantra in Tibet

A Human Approach to World Peace

Opening the Eye of New Awareness

Kindness, Clarity, and Insight

*The Dalai Lama at Harvard, Lectures on
the Buddhist Path to Peace*

Universal Responsibility and the Good Heart

The Opening of the Wisdom Eye

*The World of Tibetan Buddhism: An Overview
of its Philosophy and Practice*

MY LAND
AND
MY PEOPLE

The Original Autobiography

of His Holiness the

DALAI LAMA OF TIBET

WARNER BOOKS

NEW YORK   BOSTON

Warner Books Edition
Copyright © 1962 by His Holiness the Dalai Lama of Tibet
Copyright © renewed 1990 by His Holiness the Dalai Lama of Tibet
Introduction copyright © 1997 by His Holiness the Dalai Lama of Tibet
Foreword copyright © 1997 by Melissa Mathison Ford
All rights reserved.

Warner Books

Time Warner Book Group
1271 Avenue of the Americas, New York, NY 10020
Visit our Web site at www.twbookmark.com.

Printed in the United States of America
First Warner Books Edition: December 1997
10 9 8 7

Library of Congress Cataloging-in-Publication Data
Bstan-'dzin-rgya-mtsho, Dalai Lama XIV
    My land and my people : the original autobiography of His Holiness the Dalai Lama of Tibet / the Dalai Lama of Tibet.
        p. cm.
    Originally published: New York : Potala Corp., 1977
    Includes bibliographical references.
    ISBN 0-446-67421-4
    1. Bstan-'dzin-rgya-mtsho, Dalai Lama XIV, 1935- 2. Dalai lamas—Biography. 3. Tibet (China)—History. I. Title.
BQ7935.B777A3 1997
294.3'923'092—dc21
[B]   97-23849
                                                                          CIP

Book design by Charles Sutherland
Cover design by Diane Luger
Cover photograph by Jessica Tempas/Scott Rodgers.

INTRODUCTION

I am very pleased to write this introduction for the Warner Books reissue of my autobiography *My Land and My People*. Published in 1962, it was first written in Tibetan and then translated into English and subsequently translated into many other languages. Although it has been available in various editions—and my life story retold in several biographies and an updated autobiography—this book remains an important document of my early life in Tibet, the events that led to the Tibetan uprising of 1959, and my flight into exile. The sense of immediacy and urgency in my writing then would be difficult to re-create today.

When I and my fellow Tibetans first became refugees, the goodwill and the generosity of the Indian people and the Government of India provided the foundation on which we were able to start our lives anew. Nepal, Bhutan, and Sikkim also gave asylum and assistance, for which we are grateful. Among those who came forward to help, Christian church groups and the Swiss were the most generous and consistent throughout the rehabilitation process. Since then, whole communities have been built in exile with agricultural settlements, handicraft centers, schools, monasteries, and institutions of higher learning and research to preserve the literary, medical, and artistic heritage of Tibet. Indeed, Tibetan exiles have emerged from the difficult and trying early years to become one of the most successfully resettled refugee groups in the world.

Despite the apparent success as refugees, however, Tibetan exiles have never forgotten the primary purpose of leaving Tibet—to fight for our freedom. Today, there are over 130,000 Tibetan exiles. Approximately 10 percent of these live outside the Indian subcontinent with the largest groups in Switzerland, Canada, and the United States—countries that offered special immigration opportunities. The exile community has become an international one that remains committed to the cause of Tibet in a nonviolent manner. It maintains close ties with Tibet and actively participates in the struggle through local and international groups, and through a democratically elected parliament and government-in-exile.

During the early years of exile, when we were struggling to survive as a people and trying to preserve our identity and culture, the situation in Tibet was getting worse every year. The process of death and destruction, which had begun in the 1950s, escalated during the chaos of the Cultural Revolution. When it was all over, some 6,400 (99.9 percent) monasteries had been destroyed, and roughly 1,200,000 (out of a total of approximately 6 million) Tibetans had died prematurely as a direct result of Chinese occupation policies.

In 1979, after Deng Xiaoping had brought an end to the Cultural Revolution, he took the personal initiative to communicate with me, and in a brief message stated that short of independence for Tibet—or separation from the motherland as he called it—he was open to discussing all outstanding issues. I responded positively, and between 1979

and 1984 we were able to send four fact-finding delegations
into Tibet and two delegations to begin discussions in Beijing. This brief period was one of considerable hope, and
conditions in Tibet improved as well. However, with raised
expectations, the Tibetan people began to show their frus-
tration at the pace of progress. There were demonstrations
in Lhasa and other parts of Tibet, to which the Chinese responded forcefully and even imposed martial law. Shortly
thereafter Beijing too was engulfed by demonstrations for
greater freedoms, ending in a harsher crackdown and the im-
position of martial law once again. The climate changed and
the newfound Chinese openness came to a sudden halt.

While it is true that the Chinese leadership has failed to
understand the true nature of the Tibetan issue and we have
all lost valuable time during these years, the present draw-
back does not disappoint me completely. I am optimistic that
gradual and positive changes will take place in China in the
near future. I have often stated clearly and publicly that I
am not asking for the independence of Tibet. While Tibet
was historically an independent and separate nation from
China, I am aware of the possibility that, in a changing
world, a smaller community or nation could benefit by being
associated with a larger state. I do not want to debate history; I want to look to the future. Concerns over military
and foreign matters, which I assume are high on the list of
the Chinese, can be handled by Beijing. What is essential is
that the Tibetans have genuine self-rule.

I have detailed these ideas and conveyed them to the Chinese leadership in Beijing, and I have made them public as
well. While some Tibetans have criticized these proposals
in very severe terms, I am personally committed to them
and feel that this is the best possible nonviolent way in which
to serve the Tibetan people and nation. The essence of these
plans also calls for a genuine democratic form of government for the Tibetan people, and for Tibet to be gradually
transformed into a zone of "Ahimsa," a zone of nonconflict.

I have suggested that this can be achieved initially by removing military forces from civilian areas, and eventually by removing all military personnel and arms by agreement with concerned parties. My belief is that the absence of armaments and military personnel will practically eliminate the possibility of any conflict in the region among all parties, particularly between the larger powers such as India and China. This is how I believe Tibet, as a zone of peace, can truly contribute to peace in the region and in the world.

Unfortunately, a positive and timely response from the Chinese has not been forthcoming. On the other hand, the official reaction to my confirmation of the reincarnation of the Panchen Lama, a quintessential Tibetan practice that is religious and traditional, has been swift and unusually strong and negative. Nevertheless, despite the lack of progress on the official front, I am encouraged by the response from the Chinese people—scholars, intellectuals, writers, thinkers, and democracy activists—who in recent years, concerned with developments in Tibet, have called on Beijing to open negotiations with me. In March 1994, fifty-four prominent citizens of Shanghai, in an appeal to Beijing on many issues, included a call for the government to initiate dialogue with me, and in 1996 a democracy activist from Guangzhou and a history teacher from Beijing University made a similar suggestion. Many other dissidents have also spoken up, including Wei Jinshen, who is renowned for his very detailed references to Tibet and for his call to the Chinese government to resolve the outstanding issues. Chinese scholars abroad have also tried to offer their solutions to the Tibetan problem: a few years ago, in a conference on the future of China the deliberations focused on the need for a new constitution and called for a Confederated China that not only granted Tibet confederal status but even recognized the right of the Tibetans to break away completely in the future. The fact that these Chinese scholars have clearly recognized the independent status of Tibet and the rights of the Tibetan people encourages me tremendously. How can China remain in-different, ignore international opinion, and disregard the voices of her own best minds?

My recent visit to Taiwan was also most encouraging. It confirmed my belief that an economically vibrant society need not be at odds with a robust democracy and that there can be genuine warmth and friendship between the Tibetans and the Chinese peoples. These are some of the obvious reasons that give me hope that changes for the better will happen in the near future for Tibet.

In my travels within India and the rest of the world, I have become more and more convinced of the fundamental need of all human beings to seek greater happiness and to avoid any suffering. And, as the world becomes smaller with the advancement of science and technology and increasingly interdependent economically, what happens in one part of the world no longer remains an isolated issue, but has an impact globally.

In such a world, I believe that all the different religious traditions have an important role to play, and irrespective of the philosophical differences, which can often be basic and fundamental, they teach us the value of love and compassion, and how to be a better person with a warm heart. In my limited capacity as a Buddhist monk, I have tried to contribute to this idea by showing my respect to all the different spiritual traditions of the world by stressing our commonality, and by opening a dialogue on advancing our goals to create a better human being and a better world. Through my sincere participation in many interfaith services and interreligious dialogues we may have made some modest progress. And I have no doubt that we have all learned a lot by sharing the experience and insight of each other's contemplative, philosophical, meditative, and mystical traditions and techniques.

It is my strong belief that human beings need love and compassion for our fullest development and genuine happiness. When we are born we need the love and compassion of our parents and when we are old we are once again dependent on the love and compassion of others. With a proper sense of compassion and love, we can clearly see that the desire of others—for peace and happiness, and the avoidance of suffering—is just the same as one's own. That is why the promotion of compassion will help us to reduce the possibilities of war, help us to share the natural resources of the world in a more equitable manner, and teach us to take care of the environment. That is also why I speak up for the universal upkeep of the principles of human rights, based on the ideas of compassion. These are not Western ideas, as some totalitarian and military rulers in Asia have conveniently suggested to justify their disregard of human rights and their lack of fairness over whom they rule. These are simple universal truths. We all have a special responsibility to help create a better world, because material progress alone is clearly insufficient for a happier human society. No one loses, and everyone gains by a shared universal sense of responsibility to this planet and all living things on it.

Another reason why I am optimistic is because many totalitarian societies, societies in which the freedoms and the rights of an individual were often considered secondary to the collective good, have now begun to transform themselves into more democratic and humane institutions. And I am grateful that the East-West conflict, which kept us on the brink of possible nuclear destruction, has now receded into the background. In particular, I am most impressed by the manner in which apartheid has ended in South Africa, and by the progress that is being made in the Middle East. I am impressed because these seemingly insoluble problems have been brought to some stages of conclusion through dialogue and discussion.

But I am most encouraged by the growing worldwide concern and support for the Tibetan cause: Tens of thousands of individual citizens from all walks of life—musicians, artists, scholars, writers—and hundreds of Tibet support groups have joined us in our struggle for freedom and life in Tibet. It is also reflected in the gestures of solidarity from entire legislative bodies in many parts of the world, especially the United States Congress and the European Parliament, who have provided the leadership. Correct information about Tibet and the growing understanding of the cultural value of Tibet has contributed to this, and the Nobel Peace Prize, which I received in 1989, should be acknowledged for advancing this greater awareness of Tibet all over the world.

I remain determined and committed to the basic idea that the cultural and religious traditions of Tibet must be saved, and that freedom for the Tibetans also be secured, not just for ourselves, but for the world. And, as I continue to reach out to the Chinese leadership, I want to say again that the Tibetan struggle is not against the Chinese people or China, but an effort to protect and advance the legitimate rights of the Tibetan people, and to save a rich and valuable cultural heritage of the world.

—His Holiness the Dalai Lama

FOREWORD

I purchased a copy of *My Land and My People* in a small bookshop in London about seventeen or eighteen years ago. I had the slimmest of introductions to Tibet and the Dalai Lama. I had read Sir Charles Bell's *Biography of a Dalai Lama* about the Thirteenth and I had studied Chinese history in school, but that was the sixties. We liked Mao then. The depiction of Tibet readily available in the pro-Red China era was prejudiced and incorrect.

Sometime during the making of the movie *E.T.* an idea began to take root. I wanted to write a movie about the Fourteenth Dalai Lama. His story was remarkable. His story was "the" story for me: a boy, plucked from obscurity, was nurtured and schooled, isolated and loved. He was invested with all that was good about His people, and then, just as He was on the threshold of manhood, the boy was asked to save His country. It was *Prince and the Pauper*. There was something Greek about His story, no doubt. Something godlike.

I asked for permission to write and permission was granted.

My husband, Harrison Ford, and I first met His Holiness in Santa Barbara, California, in 1991 at the Red Lion Inn. We pitched the movie. It was hilarious. I was a nervous wreck. But, of course, His Holiness was sublime. He understood precisely what I wished to achieve. (I think He knew then what I would discover in the story, much more than I did.)

His Holiness asked, "How long will it take?" "One year to research and write," I answered. "One year to get someone to make the movie. One year to make and release. Three years." His Holiness thought. He said, "Four. Five." It will be seven by the time *Kundun* opens: the seven most interesting, eye-opening, enlightening years of my life. In those years I have come to know Tibet and Tibetans, and, ever so slightly, His Holiness the Dalai Lama.

His story is still "the" story. But here is the second act: the boy became a refugee. In the twentieth century, who has a clearer concept of our world culture, our world dharma, our world karma than the refugee? We are honored and blessed to live in a time when the Buddha is with us and He is a refugee.

I am looking forward to the third act in this remarkable life. I believe it will have a happy ending. I believe the Dalai Lama will return to Tibet, having saved His country, having completed the task set before Him in childhood. If He does not, we will all share in the blame. But if He does, we all share in the glory.

—Melissa Mathison Ford
May 1997

Melissa Mathison Ford is a writer who has written the screenplays for the films *E.T., The Black Stallion, The Indian in the Cupboard*, and *Kundun*. She lives in Jackson, Wyoming, with her husband and two children.

CONTENTS

▣ 1 ▣

THE FARMER'S SON

I was born in a small village called Taktser, in the north-east of Tibet, on the fifth day of the fifth month of the Wood Hog Year of the Tibetan calendar—that is, in 1935. Taktser is in the district called Dokham, and that name is descriptive, for *Do* means the lower part of a valley that merges into the plains, and *Kham* is the eastern part of Tibet where the distinctive race of Tibetans called Khampa lives. Thus Dokham is the part of Tibet where our mountains begin to descend to the plains of the east, towards China. Taktser itself is about 9,000 feet above the sea.

It was beautiful country. Our village, which lay on a little plateau, was almost encircled by fertile fields of wheat and barley; and the plateau, in turn, was surrounded by ranges of hills which were covered by grass—thick and vividly green.

To the south of the village there was a mountain which was higher than the rest. Its name was Ami-chiri, but the local people also called it The Mountain which Pierces the

Sky, and it was regarded as the abode of the guardian deity of the place. Its lower slopes were covered by forests; above them a rich growth of grass could be seen; higher still, the rock was bare; and on the summit was a patch of snow which never melted. On the northern face of the mountain there were junipers and poplars, peaches, plums and walnuts, and many kinds of berries and scented flowers. Clear springs of water fell in cascades, and the birds and the wild animals—deer, wild asses, monkeys, and a few leopards, bears and foxes—all wandered unafraid of man; for our people were Buddhists who would never willingly harm a living creature.

Amid the splendor of this natural beauty stood the monastery called Karma Shar Tsong Ridro, which is a famous place in the religious history of Tibet. It was founded by Karma Rolpai Dorje, the fourth reincarnation of Karmapa, who himself was the first incarnation recognized in Tibet; and it was at this monastery that our great reformer Tsongkhapa was initiated as a monk in the fourteenth century of the Christian era. Lower down was a second monastery, called Amdo Jhakyung, magnificent against the background of the mountain. The gilded roofs and the emblem called *dharma chakra* (Wheel of Religion), supported by deer of copper and gold on either side, not only added to the color of the scene, but gave an air of sanctity to the whole of the neighborhood. And this air was enhanced by the prayer flags on the roofs of all the houses in the village.

Taktser was a farming community and the staple foods of its people were wheat flour and *tsampa*—which is a kind of barley meal—and meat and butter; and their drinks were buttered tea and a beer called *chhang,* which is made from barley. There are different opinions among Buddhists about eating meat, but it was a necessity for most Tibetans. In most of Tibet the climate was rigorous, and although food was plentiful it was very limited in variety, so it was impossible to stay healthy without eating meat—and the custom had lingered there since before Buddhism was brought to the country. Tibetans would think it a sin to kill any animal, for any reason, but they did not think it sinful to go to market and buy the meat of an animal which was already dead. The butchers who slaughtered the animals were regarded as sinners and outcasts.

The surplus barley and wheat at Taktser were sold in the nearest towns—Kumbum and Sining—in exchange for tea, sugar, cotton cloth, ornaments, and iron utensils. The people's dress was purely Tibetan: The men wore fur caps and high leather boots, and the kind of cloak which was seen in different varieties all over Tibet—belted rather below the waist and hanging above it in folds which were convenient as pockets. The women wore long sleeveless woolen dresses with bright blouses of cotton or silk, and on every special occasion long ornate headdresses which hung down to their waists at the back. In winter everyone used fur coats and clothes with thick fleecy linings. Like their sisters in any other part of the world, the women of Taktser liked jewels and precious stones; but it was more the pride of the men of the village that the women were excellent cooks.

There were many other monasteries and many temples in the neighborhood, where anybody could pray and make offerings—whether he were a monk or not. Indeed, the whole life of the place was based on its religion. There was hardly anyone in the whole of Tibet who was not a faithful Buddhist. Even children, so young they could hardly talk, enjoyed paying visits to places where emblems of the Three Jewels—Buddha, Dharma, and Sanga—were kept. Children also played at building temples of clay, arranging offerings before them, and making gestures of worship which they seemed to know by instinct without being taught. Everybody, rich or poor (except a few misers) spent all his spare income—after buying the physical necessities of life—in building religious monuments, contributing to temples, making offerings to the Three Jewels, giving alms to the poor, and saving the lives of animals by buying them from the butchers.

Well-to-do householders always had a shrine in their homes where several monks were given food in return for perpetual prayers; and sometimes such a person would invite hundreds of monks to recite from holy texts for days at a time, and pay and feed them well for doing so. Even the poorest people had a little altar and an image of Lord Buddha in their cottages, where butter lamps were always kept lighted.

So although the people of Dokham were mostly tall and strong, and hardy and brave by nature, those qualities were tempered to gentleness by their faith. Humility and charity, temperance, kindness, affection and consideration for all other beings: these were the virtues encouraged by their beliefs.

It was among such amiable people that I was born in a family of pure Tibetan stock. Although my family had settled in Dokham, my forefathers came from central Tibet. How they came to settle in eastern Tibet is a simple story. Hundreds of years ago, in the reign of King Mangsong Mangtsen, a Tibetan army was stationed in the northeastern part of Tibet to protect the frontiers. In our part of Dokham, a garrison from Phempo in central Tibet was stationed, and family tradition said that my forefathers came with that garrison. In our family dialect we still used many words from the Phempo district, rather than from the east: words like *cheney* for bowl and *khenbu* for spoon. Except for the last two generations, a member of my family had always been the headman of our village, with the title of Chhija Nangso: *Chhija* was a name of the place, and *Nangso* means the "inner watchman." I have always been glad that I come from a humble family of peasants. I left my village when I was very young, as I shall tell, but years later, when I was on my way back from China, I paid a hurried visit to Taktser, and I could not help feeling a sense of pride when I saw my ancestral village and my home. I have always felt that if I had been born in a rich or aristocratic family I would not have been able to appreciate the feelings and sentiments of the humble classes of Tibetans. But owing to my lowly birth, I can understand them and read their minds, and that is why I feel for them so strongly and have tried my best to improve their lot in life.

Our family was large, for I have two sisters and four brothers—and we are widely spread out in age. My mother gave birth to sixteen children, but nine of them died when they were very young. The whole family was linked together by the strongest bonds of love and kindness. My father himself was a very kind-hearted man. He was rather short-tempered too, but his anger never lasted long. He was not very tall or strong, and he was not highly educated, but he had natural cleverness and intelligence. He was especially fond of horses and used to ride a great deal, and he had a talent for choosing good horses and for healing them when they were sick. My mother is a kind and loving person. She feels for everyone; she will gladly give her own meal to a hungry person, and go hungry herself. Yet although she is so gentle, she always ruled the family. She is also adaptable and farsighted, so that after my installation had opened up new possibilities for us, she made it her special duty to see that her other children were properly educated.

Our main livelihood was in agriculture, but we also kept cattle and horses and grew vegetables in our garden. Normally, we had five workers on our farm, and much of the work was done by the family, but during the sowing and harvesting season for a few days we had to hire from fifteen to forty men who were paid in kind. And in our village there existed the custom of helping each other whenever a family stood in need of help or found itself in any difficulty. When my mother went out to work in the fields while I was a baby, she used to carry me on her back, and leave me to sleep in a corner of the field under an umbrella tied to a stake in the ground.

Our house was a square building with a courtyard in the middle. It was single-storied, with the lower part built of stone and the upper part of earth. The edges of the flat roof were lined with turquoise tiles. The main gate faced the south, towards Ami-chiri, and the top of the gate was decorated with spears and flags in the manner which is traditional in Tibet. Prayer flags fluttered from the top of a tall pole in the middle of the courtyard. At the back of the house was a yard where our horses and mules and cattle were kept, and in front of the gate a Tibetan mastiff was tied to a post to guard the house against intruders.

The cattle were eight cows and seven *dzomos,* which are crosses between yaks and cows. (The word *yak* means only the male animal, like the word bull. The female of a yak is a *dri.)* My mother used to milk the *dzomos* herself, and as soon as I learned to walk I used to follow her out to the barn, with my bowl in the fold of my gown, and she would give me milk warm from the *dzomo.* We had chickens too, and I was allowed to go to the henhouse to collect the eggs. This must be one of my earliest recollections. I remember climbing into one of the nesting boxes and sitting there clucking like a hen.

The life of our family was simple, but it was happy and content, and much of its contentment was owed to Thupten Gyatso, the Thirteenth Dalai Lama, who had been the spiritual and temporal ruler of Tibet for many years. During his rule, he had clarified and defined the status of Tibet as an independent nation, and he had also achieved a great deal for the betterment of his people. The eastern district where we lived was under the secular rule of China, but he was its spiritual leader, and he had lived there for nearly a year, so that the people were directly under his influence. He said in a testament he addressed to all his people: "After I took up the duties of spiritual and secular administration, there was no leisure for me, no time for pleasure. Day and night I had to ponder anxiously over problems of religion and state, in order to decide how each might prosper best. I had to consider the welfare of the peasantry, how best to remove their sorrows and how to open the three doors of Promptitude, Impartiality, and Justice."

Through his devotion, the people of Tibet had begun to enjoy a long era of peace and prosperity. He himself had said: "From that year, the Year of the Water Bull, to this present Water Monkey Year, this land of Tibet has been happy and prosperous. It is like a land made new. All the people are at ease and happy."

But in the Year of the Water Bird, that is, in 1933, Thupten Gyatso departed from this world, and as the news spread through Tibet, the people were desolate. It was my father who brought the sad news to our village; he had been to market in Kumbum and heard it in the great monastery there. The Thirteenth Dalai Lama had done so much for the peace and welfare of Tibet that the people decided to build a golden mausoleum of special magnificence as a token of their homage and respect. By ancient custom, this splendid tomb was erected inside the Potala Palace in Lhasa, the capital of Tibet.

With the passing of the Thirteenth Dalai Lama, the search began at once for his reincarnation, for each Dalai Lama is a reincarnation of his predecessor. The first, who was born in the year 1391 of the Christian era, was an incarnation of Chenresi, the Buddha of Mercy, who made a vow to protect all living beings.

First, a Regent had to be appointed by the National Assembly to govern the country until the new reincarnation could be found and grow to maturity. Then, in accordance with the time-honored customs and traditions, the state oracles and learned lamas were consulted—as a first step towards finding out where the reincarnation had appeared. Curious cloud formations were seen in the northeast from

Lhasa. It was recalled that after the Dalai Lama died, his body was placed seated on a throne in the Norbulingka, his summer residence in Lhasa, facing towards the south; but after a few days it was seen that the face had turned towards the east. And on a wooden pillar on the northeastern side of the shrine where the body sat, a great star-shaped fungus suddenly appeared. All this and other evidence indicated the direction where the new Dalai Lama should be sought.

Next, in 1935, the Tibetan Wood Hog Year, the Regent went to the sacred lake of Lhamoi Latso at Chokhorgyal, about ninety miles southeast of Lhasa. The people of Tibet believe that visions of the future can be seen in the waters of this lake. There are many such holy lakes in Tibet, but Lhamoi Latso is the most celebrated of them all. Sometimes the visions are said to appear in the form of letters, and sometimes as pictures of places and future events. Several days were spent in prayers and meditation, and then the Regent saw the vision of three Tibetan letters—*Ah, Ka* and *Ma,*—followed by a picture of a monastery with roofs of jade green and gold and a house with turquoise tiles. A detailed description of these visions was written down and kept a strict secret.

In the following year, high lamas and dignitaries, carrying the secrets of the visions, were sent out to all parts of Tibet to search for the place which the Regent had seen in the waters.

The wise men who went to the east arrived in our region of Dokham during the winter, and they observed the green and golden roofs of the monastery of Kumbum. In the village of Taktser, they noticed at once a house with turquoise tiles. Their leader asked if the family living in the house had any children and was told that they had a boy who was nearly two years old.

On hearing this significant news, two members of the party went to the house in disguise, together with a servant and two local monastic officials who were acting as their guides. A junior monastic official of the main party, whose name was Losang Tsewang, pretended to be the leader, while the real leader, Lama Kewtsang Rinpoché of Sera Monastery, was dressed in poor clothes and acted as a servant. At the gate of the house, the strangers were met by my parents, who invited Losang into the house, believing him to be the master, while the lama and the others were received in the servants' quarters. There they found the baby of the family, and the moment the little boy saw the lama, he went to him and wanted to sit on his lap. The lama was disguised in a cloak which was lined with lambskin, but round his neck he was wearing a rosary which had belonged to the Thirteenth Dalai Lama. The little boy seemed to recognize the rosary, and he asked to be given it. The lama promised to give it to him if he could guess who he was, and the boy replied that he was *Sera-aga,* which meant, in the local dialect, "a lama of Sera." The lama asked who the "master" was, and the boy gave the name of Losang. He also knew the name of the real servant, which was Amdo Kasang.

The lama spent the whole day in watching the little boy with increasing interest, until it was time for the boy to be put to bed. All the party stayed in the house for the night, and early next morning, when they were making ready to leave, the boy got out of his bed and insisted that he wanted to go with them.

I was that boy.

So far, my mother and father had not suspected the real mission of the travelers they had entertained, but a few days later the whole search party of senior lamas and high dignitaries came to our house in Taktser. At the sight of this large distinguished party of visitors, my mother and father understood that I might be a reincarnation, for there are many incarnate lamas in Tibet, and my elder brother had already proved to be one of them. An incarnate lama had recently died at the monastery of Kumbum, and they thought the visitors might be searching for his reincarnation, but it did not occur to them that I might be the reincarnation of the Dalai Lama himself.

It is common for small children who are reincarnations to remember objects and people from their previous lives. Some can also recite the scriptures although they have not yet been taught them. All I had said to the lama had suggested to him that he might at last have discovered the reincarnation he was seeking. The whole party had come to make further tests. They brought with them two identical black rosaries, one of which had belonged to the Thirteenth Dalai Lama. When they offered them both to me, I took the one which was his and—so I am told—put it round my own neck. The same test was made with two yellow rosaries. Next, they offered me two drums, a very small drum which the Dalai Lama had used for calling attendants, and a larger and much more ornate and attractive drum with golden straps. I chose the little drum, and began to beat it in the way that drums are beaten during prayers. Last they presented two walking sticks. I touched the wrong walking stick, then paused and looked at it for some time, and then I took the other, which had belonged to the Dalai Lama, and held it in my hand. And later, when they wondered at my hesitation, they found that the first walking stick had also been used at one time by the Dalai Lama, and that he had given it to a lama who in turn had given it to Kewtsang Rinpoché.

By these tests, they were further convinced that the reincarnation had been found, and their conviction was strengthened by the vision of three letters which the Regent had seen in the lake. They believed that the first letter, *Ah*, stood for Amdo, which was the name of our district. *Ka* could have stood for Kumbum, which was one of the largest monasteries in the neighborhood, and the one which the Regent had seen in the vision; or the two letters *Ka* and *Ma* might have signified the monastery of Karma Rolpai Dorje on the mountain above the village.

It also seemed to them to be significant that some years before, the Thirteenth Dalai Lama had stayed at the monastery of Karma Rolpai Dorje, when he was on his way back from China. He had been welcomed there by the incarnate lama of the monastery, and received homage and obeisance from the people of the village, including my father, who was nine years old at the time. It was also recalled that the Dalai Lama had left a pair of his boots or *jachhen* behind at the monastery. He had also looked for some time at the house where I was born, and remarked that it was a beautiful place.

By all these facts, the search party was fully convinced that the reincarnation was discovered. They reported all the details to Lhasa by telegram. There was only one telegraph line in Tibet, from Lhasa to India, and so the message had to be sent in code from Sining through China and India; and by the same route an order came back to take me at once to the Holy City.

However, since the northeastern part of Tibet where we lived was under Chinese control at that time, the Chinese governor had first to be consulted. The search party told him they had come to seek for the new Dalai Lama and asked for his help in taking possible candidates to Lhasa. They did not tell him they believed they had made the final choice, for fear that he might make difficulties. And in fact, he would not give an answer. He twice summoned all the boys he was told had been considered, and although he himself was a Moslem, he decided to make a test of his own. It was a very simple test. He offered a box of sweets to us all. Some of the boys were too frightened to take any, and some were so greedy that they took a handful, but I, I am told, took one and ate it discreetly. This, and some questioning, seemed to satisfy him that I was the likeliest choice, for he sent all the other children home, presenting a roll of cloth to each of their parents, but to my parents he gave orders to take me to the monastery of Kumbum and leave me there in the charge of my brother—who was already a monastic student.

It is said that the Governor then demanded a ransom of a hundred thousand Chinese dollars from the representatives of the Tibetan government before he would let me go. This was a great deal of money, and he had no right to it. They paid him, but then he demanded another three hundred thousand. The government representatives told him it was still uncertain whether I was really the reincarnation, and explained that there were other candidates from other parts of Tibet. They were now afraid that if he believed I was certain to be accepted as the Dalai Lama, he would put his price even higher, and cause even more delay. They also felt there was a danger that the Chinese government might take the opportunity to demand some kind of authority in Tibet.

These difficulties had to be referred to Lhasa. It seemed unwise to discuss them in telegrams through China, so messages had to be sent to the capital by hand. It took several months to get a reply and altogether very nearly two years passed from the beginning of the search to the end of these negotiations with the Governor.

All this time, strict secrecy was observed on the whole matter, not only for fear of what the Chinese governor might do, but also because the discovery had not yet been laid before the National Assembly of Tibet for official acceptance. Not even my parents were told of the firm belief of the search party, and even through the long period of waiting they never suspected that I might be the reincarnation of the highest of all lamas. However, my mother has told me since I grew up that there had been previous signs of some extraordinary fate for me. There is a widespread superstition in Tibet that before a high incarnate lama is reborn, the district where he is born will suffer. For four years before I was born, the crops had failed in Taktser either through hailstorms when the corn was ripe, or through drought when it was young, and the village people had been saying that an incarnation must be going to be born among them. And my own family especially had fallen on hard times. Several of our horses and cattle, which were among our few valuable possessions, had died, and my father could not discover any reason. And in the few months before I was born, my father himself had been badly ill and unable to get out of bed. Yet on the morning of my birth, he got up feeling perfectly well, and offered prayers and filled the butter lamps which always burned on our family altar. My mother remembers being annoyed at this and accusing him of having stayed in bed through laziness, but he declared that he was cured. When I was born, and my mother told him, "It's a boy," he simply said, "Good. I would like to make him a monk."

While the discussions with the Governor were going on, I was left in the monastery. I was about three by then, and of course I was very unhappy at first at being separated from my parents. Beside my eldest brother, Thubten Jigme Norbu, my third brother, Losang Samten, who was five, was also there, but he had begun to take lessons, and while he was with his tutor I had nobody to play with. I still remember waiting impatiently outside his classroom, and sometimes peering round the curtain in the doorway to try to attract his attention without letting his tutor see me. But the tutor was strict, and Samten was helpless.

Our uncle was also there, and I am sorry to say that Samten and I had a childish dislike of him—mainly, I think, because he had a dark spotty face and a bristly black beard (which is rare among Tibetans) and a moustache which he carefully trained by frequent applications of fat. Also, he was often cross with us—probably not without reason. I remember his exceptionally large and ostentatious rosary, in which the beads were quite black from constant use. And I specially remember his set of loose-leaf scriptures, because once I tried to look at it and got the loose leaves all mixed up, thus earning a few sound slaps from that angry uncle. When that sort of thing happened, Samten and I used to run away and hide and leave our uncle to search for us for hours. We did not realize what intense anxiety this must have caused him, in view of the value which the Governor had placed upon me. But such escapades proved effective, for when he found us, negotiations used to take place for better relations in the future, and with luck he would pacify us with sweets— which he never gave us while we behaved ourselves.

Altogether, that was a lonely and rather unhappy phase in my childhood. Sometimes Samten's tutor used to put me on his lap and wrap me in his gown and give me dried fruits, and that is almost the only solace I remember. My sister reminds me that one of my solitary games was playing at starting on journeys: making up parcels, and then setting off with them on a hobbyhorse.

But at last, about the beginning of the sixth month of the Earth Hare Year, corresponding to 1939, the time came for my real journey to begin. The government representatives had not been able to find all the three hundred thousand dollars in cash, but luckily there were some Chinese Moslem merchants who wanted to go to Lhasa as the first stage of their pilgrimage to Mecca, and they agreed to lend the remainder of the money and to be repaid in Lhasa. Then the Chinese Governor agreed to let me go, on condition that a senior official was left behind as hostage for a set of scriptures written in gold and a complete set of the Thirteenth Dalai Lama's clothes, which he claimed should be sent to Kumbum if I safely arrived in Lhasa. This was agreed upon, but I am rather glad to say that after I did reach Lhasa there was some political trouble in Dokham, and while it was going on, the hostage escaped and also came safely to Lhasa.

We set off a week after my fourth birthday, on a journey which was to last for three months and thirteen days. It was a sad moment for my parents to leave Taktser, their home, their farm, and their friends, because they still did not know what the future held for us. There were roughly fifty people and 350 horses and mules in the caravan when it started, including the members of the search party, my own family, and the party of Moslems on their even longer pilgrimage. My parents brought two of my elder brothers with them— Gyelo Thondup, who was nine, and Losang Samten, who by then was six. There were no wheeled carts or carriages in Tibet, and no roads for them. Samten and I rode in a carriage called a *treljam,* which is attached to two poles and carried on the backs of two mules. On rough and dangerous parts of the track, the members of the search party carried me in turns. Every day, we traveled only from dawn till noon, which is the usual practice on journeys in Tibet, and every night we camped in tents, because there were very few habitations on the route. Indeed, in the early part of the journey we saw nobody for week after week, except a few nomads who came to ask me for my blessing.

As soon as I was safely out of the Chinese control, the National Assembly was convened in Lhasa to agree on a proclamation. A detailed report was submitted to the Assembly of the visions seen by the Regent, the tests which I had stood successfully, and the indications which the Thirteenth Dalai Lama had given of the place where he wanted to be reborn. It was pointed out that the search and investigation was all in accord with the advice of the leading oracles and lamas; and finally the Assembly unanimously confirmed that I was the reincarnation of the Dalai Lama, and senior officials were dispatched to meet me on the way.

We met the first of these officials at the river called Thutopchu when we were almost three months on our way. He had ten men with him, and a hundred loads of provisions, and also four skin coracles to take us and our own provisions across the river. So the caravan began to grow.

A few days later we crossed the pass called Tra-tsang-la and reached the town of Bumchen, which was fifteen days' march from Lhasa. There we were welcomed by another emissary of the government, and he offered me not only scarves, which are the universal symbol of Tibetan greeting, but also the *Mendel Tensum,* a threefold offering of reverence and homage. And it was at this moment that my father and mother first knew for certain that their youngest son was the reincarnation of the Dalai Lama, and they felt great joy and awe and thankfulness, and, for the moment, incredulity—the kind of disbelief which often comes with great and happy news.

A little farther on, ten stages out from Lhasa, we met a party of about a hundred men with many more horses and mules. This was led by a minister of the Tibetan Cabinet, and included many officials and representatives of Lhasa's three outstanding monasteries, all of whom offered me the traditional scarves and the *Mendel Tensum.* They had brought with them a proclamation declaring me to be the Fourteenth Dalai Lama, which had been issued with the authority of the Regent, the Cabinet and the National Assembly of Tibet. Then I put off my peasant clothes and was dressed in monastic robes. Ceremonial attendants were put at my service, and henceforth I was carried in a gilded palanquin known to us Tibetans as the *phebjam.*

From here, the procession advanced on an ever grander scale. In every village and town we passed, we encountered processions of lamas and monks carrying emblems and decorations. The people of these places also joined in the processions, while horns and flutes and drums and cymbals sounded, and clouds of smoke rose from incense burners. Everyone, layman or monk, was dressed in his best clothes and welcomed me with folded hands and a happy smile on his face, as I passed through the throngs. Looking out from my palanquin, I remember seeing people shedding tears of joy. Music and dancing followed me everywhere.

The next important place in our journey was Dum Uma Thang. There I was received by the Regent and the Official Abbot of Tibet, and we broke our journey and spent three days at the monastery of Rating. But the climax of the official welcome was not reached till we arrived at Döguthang. Here all the remaining senior officials were present to welcome me: the Prime Minister, the members of the Cabinet, and the leading abbots of the monasteries of Drepung, Sera, and Gaden—the three pillars of Buddhism in Tibet. I was also welcomed here by Mr. Hugh Richardson, the head of the British mission in Lhasa. We were now very close to Lhasa, and a little farther on we were met by the representatives of Bhutan, Nepal, and China. By now our party was very large, and we marched on in a long procession towards the Holy City. On both sides of our route thousands of monks were lined up in rows with colored banners. Many groups of people were singing songs of welcome and playing musical instruments. The soldiers of all the regiments of the Tibetan army were drawn up to present arms to me. The whole population of Lhasa, men and women, young and old, thronged together in their best clothes to receive and welcome me with homage. As they watched me passing, I could hear them crying, "The day of our happiness has come." I felt as if I were in a dream. I felt as if I were in a great park covered with beautiful flowers, while soft breezes blew across it and peacocks elegantly danced before me. There was an unforgettable scent of wild flowers, and a song of freedom and happiness in the air. I had not recovered from this dream when we reached the city. I was taken to the temple, where I bowed humbly before the sacred images. Then the procession went on to the Norbulingka, the summer residence of the Dalai Lama, and I was ushered still dreaming into the splendid apartments of my predecessor.

It had been decided to hold the ceremony of *Sitringasol* soon after my arrival. This was my enthronement on the Lion Throne. The date was the fourteenth day of the first month of the Iron Dragon Year, corresponding to the year 1940. It had been fixed by the Regent, in consultation with the National Assembly, according to the advice of the State astrologers. Telegrams had been sent to the government of China, the British government of India, the King of Nepal, and the Maharajas of Bhutan and Sikkim, to tell them of the date of the enthronement.

The ceremony was held in the *Si-Shi-Phuntsok* (the Hall of All Good Deeds of the Spiritual and Temporal Worlds), in the eastern part of the Potala Palace. Here had gathered the diplomatic representatives of the neighboring countries, officials of the Tibetan government (both lay and monastic) incarnate lamas, abbots and assistant abbots of the three monasteries of Drepung, Sera, and Gaden and the members of my family. As I entered the hall I was attended by the Regent, who was my Senior Tutor, and by my Junior Tutor, members of the Cabinet, the Chief Official Abbot, and the Senior Chamberlain. There were also in attendance the Master of Robes, the Master of Religious Ceremonies, the Master of the Table, and others representing the ancient regions of Tibet. The entire company rose as I entered, and I was escorted to the Lion Throne by the Chief Abbot and the senior member of the Cabinet, while the Senior Chamberlain led the procession.

The *Sengtri* (the Lion Throne), was built in accordance with the instructions of Tibetan scriptures. It was square and made of gilded wood, supported by eight lions—two at each corner—also carved in wood. It had five square cushions on it, each covered in brocade of a different color, so that its height was six or seven feet. A table in front of it carried all the seals of office of the Dalai Lama.

The ceremony began with the chanting of special prayers by a group of the monks who lived in the Potala and were specially charged with attendance on the Dalai Lama at all religious ceremonies. They also offered symbols of auspiciousness, chanting prayers indicating their significance.

Then the Regent came forward and presented the *Mendel Tensum* to me. The essence of this was three symbolic offerings: a golden image of the Buddha of Eternal Life, a book of scriptures concerning this Buddha, and a small *chöten*—a miniature of the traditional type of memorial familiar to travelers in Tibet. They signified an appeal to me to live a long life, to expound our religion, and to have thoughts like those of the Buddhas.

Then the Regent, my Junior Tutor, and the Prime Minister presented scarves to me. I blessed the Regent and my Tutor by touching their foreheads with mine; the Prime Minister, who was a layman, I blessed by touching his head with both hands.

Then the Senior Chamberlain led a procession of retainers bringing me *droma,* a sweet-tasting herb, in a small cup and saucer both made of gold. Then *droma* was offered by other retainers to everybody present in the hall. The presentation of *droma* forms part of every ceremony in Tibet; it is a symbol of good luck. This was followed by a ceremony in which tea was offered (first to me and then to all the other people), and next sweetened rice was presented. While these ceremonial presentations were going on, two scholars from the monasteries were debating on fundamental questions of religion. When this ended, a group of boys gave a performance of mime accompanied by music. Then, again, came the debate on religious questions, and while the debate was proceeding, an offering of fruit, both fresh and dried, and of Tibetan cakes known as *khabse,* was arranged in the body of the hall.

Then the Regent offered the *Mendel Tensum* on behalf of the government of Tibet. This was an elaborate emblem of the universe, held on one side by a member of the Cabinet and on the other by the Official Abbot. The Regent explained the significance of the offering, and declared that after a long search in consultation with the oracles and high lamas, I was being installed by the government and the people of Tibet as the spiritual and temporal ruler of the State. Finally he appealed to me to decide to live a long life for the prosperity of the people of Tibet and the propagation of religion. Then followed a long procession of officials, both lay and monastic, carrying gifts to me from the government of Tibet.

There was first the presentation of the Golden Wheel and a White Conch, the symbols of spiritual and temporal power. Then came eight symbols of prosperity and happiness and seven symbols of royalty. The procession ended with an array of other gifts.

It was then my turn to bless the assembly. First the officials of the Tibetan government were blessed in the spiritual manner. The foreign representatives followed and presented scarves to me. These were personally returned by me to the representatives of the highest ranks and to the others by the Chamberlain. Various kinds of fruit which had previously been placed before me in the body of the hall were now offered to me and then distributed among the others present in the hall. Another performance of the mime followed. Then came a procession of people wearing masks and robes representing the gods and goddesses of the oceans and the heavens, chanting songs in praise of our country. Then followed four masked dancers representing the ancient Indian Acharyas, and two monk officials reciting accounts of the good years in the history of Tibet and its religion. Then there was another performance of mime. The ceremony ended with the recital by two monks of verses they had composed, praying for the long life of the Dalai Lama, the victory of religion throughout the world, and the peace and prosperity of all beings under the authority of the Dalai Lama's government. I conferred special blessings on those two monk scholars and gave them scarves in appreciation of their verses.

This brought the ceremony to an end. It had been long, and I am told that everybody present had been delighted to see how, although young, I had been able to play my part with suitable dignity and composure. After it, I proceeded to the *Phuntsok Doe-Khyel* (the Chamber of the Good Deeds of Desire). Here all the officials who had accompanied me to the hall where the Enthronement had taken place were again in attendance. All the seals of my office were presented to me, and there followed my first symbolic act of sovereignty: I fixed the seals on documents conveying orders to monasteries.

Thus, when I was four-and-a-half-years old, I was formally recognized as the Fourteenth Dalai Lama, the spiritual and temporal ruler of Tibet. To all Tibetans, the future seemed happy and secure.

⊡ 2 ⊡

THE QUEST FOR
ENLIGHTENMENT

My education began when I was six, and as I was taught
entirely by the traditional system of Tibet, I must explain
its methods and purposes. Our system has proved effective,
so far, in maintaining a fairly high moral and intellectual
standard among Tibetans, although it was established many
centuries ago. By modern standards, it has the defect of entirely ignoring the scientific knowledge of recent centuries,
but the reason for that, of course, is that Tibet remained entirely isolated until very recent times.

The basic purpose of the Tibetan system is to broaden and
cultivate the mind by a wide variety of knowledge. For the
advanced standard of secular education, the curriculum includes drama, dance and music, astrology, poetry, and composition. These are known in Tibet as the "five minor
subjects." They are not reserved for lay pupils alone, but
pupils receiving religious education can also choose one or

more of them, and most of them choose astrology and composition.

For higher education, the course includes the art of healing, Sanskrit, dialectics, arts and crafts, and metaphysics and the philosophy of religion. Of these "five higher subjects," as they are called, the last is the most important and fundamental. Together with dialectics, it is divided in turn into five branches. These, with their Sanskrit names, are *Prajnaparamita,* the Perfection of Wisdom; *Madhyamika,* the Middle Path, which urges the avoidance of extremes; *Vinaya,* the Canon of Monastic Discipline; *Abhidharma,* Metaphysics; and *Pramana,* Logic and Dialectics. Strictly speaking, the last of these is not one of the branches or scriptures, but it is included in these Five Great Treatises to emphasize the importance of logic in developing mental powers. The *Tantric* part of *Mahayana* is not included among them; it is studied separately.

This religious education is followed mainly by the monks of Tibet. It is a profound study, and effort is needed to understand its difficult subject matter.

Beside providing a pupil with information, the Tibetan system lays down various methods for developing his mental faculties. To begin with, children learn to read and write by imitating their teacher. This, of course, is a natural method which one uses all one's life. To train the memory, there are rigorous courses for learning the scriptures by heart. The third method, explanation, is used throughout the world, and some of our monastic colleges depend on it for teaching their students. But many monasteries prefer the method of dialectical discussions between pupil and teacher or between pupils alone. Finally, there are the methods of meditation and concentration, which are especially used for training the mind for the advanced study and practice of religion.

Like most children, I started by learning to read and write, and I felt what I suppose young boys of that age generally feel—a certain reluctance and some resistance. The idea of being tied down to books and the company of teachers was not very interesting. However, I found myself doing my lessons to my teachers' satisfaction, and as I got used to the strict course of study, they began to mark my progress as rather unusually rapid.

There are four different forms of Tibetan script. For the first two years, I learned from my Senior and Junior Tutors to read the form which is used for printing—it is known as *U-chhen.* At the same time I learned a verse from the scriptures by heart every day and spent another hour in reading the scriptures. Then, when I was eight, I began to learn the ordinary written form of Tibetan, which is called *U-me.* I was taught this by an old companion, Khenrab Tenzin, who had been with the search party and came back with me from Dokham to Lhasa. He was a monk official and a man of character, who had a special gift for teaching small children. He followed the method which is always used in Tibet—he wrote the Tibetan characters without any ink on a small wooden board which had been covered with chalk dust, and then I had to write over the characters with ink, beginning with large characters and later, as I progressed, writing them smaller. After a time, I began to copy words which he had written at the top of the board. For about eight months I wrote on wooden boards to acquire the proper form of script, and then Khenrab Tenzin began to allow me to write on paper. Later, my Junior Tutor, Trijang Rinpoché, taught me grammar and spelling. Altogether I spent about five years on writing Tibetan. This was in addition, of course, to my daily study of the scriptures, morning and evening, for religious training was the main purpose of my education, and reading, writing, and grammar were only a means to that end.

My religious education in dialectical discussion did not begin in earnest till I was twelve. At first it was not very easy, because I felt again a certain mental resistance, more intense than the similar experience six years earlier. But soon the difficulties disappeared, and the subjects became most agreeable. I had to study and learn by heart the treatises on the "higher subjects," and take part in discussions of them, at times debating with the most learned scholars. I began on the *Prajnaparamita* (the Perfection of Wisdom). There are over thirty volumes of commentaries on this treatise, and the monastic universities make their own choice. I chose for myself, beside the fundamental principles of the treatise, two of its commentaries, one by the great Indian Pandit Singhabhadra, and the other, consisting of 302 pages, by the Fifth Dalai Lama. Henceforth I had to learn about a third of a page by heart every day and read and understand much more. At the same time my training in the art of dialectical argument began with elementary logic. Seven learned scholars from the seven monastic colleges of the Drepung, Sera, and Gaden monasteries were selected to help me for this purpose.

When I was just over thirteen, in the eighth month of the Fire Hog Year, I was formally admitted to the two large monasteries of Drepung and Sera. On this occasion, I had to attend congregational debates at the five monastic colleges of these two monasteries. This was the first time I had taken part in public dialectical discussions on the Great Treatises, and naturally I felt shy, excited, and a little worried. My opponents were learned abbots, who were formidable contestants in debate, and the meetings were attended by hundreds of religious dignitaries, all of whom were scholars, and by thousands of monks. However, the learned lamas told me afterwards that I had conducted myself to their satisfaction.

I will not ask all my readers of other religions to follow me throughout my further studies of Buddhist thought, for Buddhism is an intellectual rather than an emotional religion, and it has a literature of thousands of volumes, of which I studied hundreds. However, I have given a short explanation of the Buddhism of Tibet in the Appendix of this book. And I will confess that when I was introduced to metaphysics and philosophy soon after I was thirteen, they unnerved me so that I had the feeling of being dazed, as though I were hit on the head by a stone. But that phase did not linger beyond the first few days, and after that the new studies, like the earlier courses, became simpler and clearer. "Nothing remains difficult once you get used to it," an Indian seer has said, and I certainly found this was so in my education. One by one, other subjects were added to my curriculum, and as I went on I found less and less difficulty in learning all that was required of me. In fact, I began to feel a growing inquisitiveness to know more and more. My interest reached beyond my allotted studies, and I found satisfaction in reading advanced chapters of the books and wanting to know from my teachers more than I was supposed to at my age.

This increase in one's intellectual powers is associated with spiritual development. At each stage in my training, I received consecration of the mind and body in preparation for the higher doctrines. I had the first of these initiations when I was eight, and I still remember it vividly, and the feeling of peace and happiness it brought me. At each of the later ceremonies, I could feel the spiritual experience which has always been associated with them. My belief and faith in my religion became deeper, the assurance in my mind that I was following the right path became firmer.

As I grew more accustomed to these experiences and reached the age of about fifteen, I was able to sense a spontaneous feeling growing within me of gratitude to Lord Buddha. I also felt an immense debt to those teachers, mostly Indians, who had given the Tibetans their invaluable religious doctrines, and to those Tibetan scholars who had interpreted and preserved them in our language. I began to think less of myself and more of others and became aware of the concept of compassion.

It was this sense of spiritual elevation which was attended

on the mental plane by a sense of improved intellect, by better powers of memory, greater proficiency in debate, and increased self-confidence.

Political and other circumstances, as I shall tell, did not allow me to carry on my studies like the scholars of great talent and learning who devote their whole lives to the pursuit of religious knowledge and spiritual enlightenment. But for a period of thirteen years I was able to give a good part of my time and attention to these serious studies, and when I was twenty-four I took the preliminary examination at each of the three monastic universities.

These examinations are always in the form of congregational debates. The rules of procedure are simple, but dignified. Each student has to face a large number of opponents who choose whatever subject and whatever disputable point they think necessary to defeat their adversary, and all the standard works of Indian and Tibetan scholars, as well as Lord Buddha's words embodied in the Sutras, are quoted to refute the contentions of the opposing party. At each of my preliminary examinations, I had to compete with fifteen learned scholars in these debates, three for each of the five treatises, and defend my thesis and refute their arguments. Then I had to stand before two very erudite abbots and initiate a dialectical discussion on any of the five principal subjects. In all these debates, strong formal gestures are made to emphasize each point, so that the arguments appear like battles of intellect, which indeed they are.

A year later, I appeared for my final examination, during the annual Monlam Festival in Lhasa, when many thousands of monks come into the city to attend the special Buddhist festival of prayer which is held in the first month of each year. This examination was held in three sessions. In the morning I was examined on *Pramana,* or logic, by thirty scholars turn by turn in congregational discussion. In the afternoon, fifteen scholars took part as my opponents in debate on *Madhyamika* (the Middle Path), and *Prajnaparamita* (the Perfection of Wisdom). In the evening there were thirty-five scholars to test my knowledge of *Vinaya,* the canon of monastic discipline, and *Abhidharma,* the study of metaphysics. And at each session hundreds of learned lamas in their brilliant red and yellow robes—my own tutors anxiously among them—and thousands of monks sat round us on the ground, eagerly and critically listening. I found these examinations extremely difficult, because I had to concentrate so hard on the subject with which I was dealing, and had to be so prompt in answering any questions. Several hours of debate seemed like an instant. Of course, I was proud and happy to be taking the final examinations and to receive the degree of Master of Metaphysics, after so many years of studying the great teachings of Lord Buddha. But I knew that there is really no end to one's need for continual learning until one can reach the highest stages of spiritual attainment.

Such a religious training, in my view, brings a certain unique equanimity of mind. The practical test comes when occasions of sorrow or suffering arise. The person whose mind is conditioned by the study and practice of religion faces these circumstances with patience and forbearance. The person who does not follow the path of religion may break under the impact of what he regards as calamities, and may end in either self-frustration, or else in pursuits which inflict unhappiness on others. Humanitarianism and true love for all beings can only stem from an awareness of the content of religion. By whatever name religion may be known, its understanding and practice are the essence of a peaceful mind and therefore of a peaceful world. If there is no peace in one's mind, there can be no peace in one's approach to others, and thus no peaceful relations between individuals or between nations.

Here I must give a brief explanation of our beliefs, and the significance of my own position as the Dalai Lama, because these beliefs had a most profound influence on all that I did and all that our people did when our time of trouble came. But I must also add that it is impossible to describe the complexities of the Buddhist doctrine in a few lines, and so I shall not try to indicate more than the general trend of it, for the sake of those to whom it is quite unfamiliar.

We believe, with good reason, that all beings of various forms (both animal and human) are reborn after death. In each life, the proportion of pain and joy which they experience is determined by their good or evil deeds in the life before, although they may modify the proportion by their efforts in their present life. This is known as the law of Karma. Beings may move up or down in the Kure realms, for example, from animal to human life or back. Finally, by virtue and enlightenment, they will achieve Nirvana, when they cease to be reborn. Within Nirvana, there are stages of enlightenment: the highest of all—the perfection of enlightenment—is Buddhahood.

Belief in rebirth should engender a universal love, for all living beings and creatures, in the course of their numberless lives and our own, have been our beloved parents, children, brothers, sisters, friends. And the virtues our creed encourages are those which arise from this universal love— tolerance, forbearance, charity, kindness, compassion.

Incarnations are beings who have either achieved various stages of Nirvana or have achieved the highest stage below Nirvana—the Buddhas, Bodhisattvas and Arahats. They are reincarnated in order to help other beings to rise toward Nirvana, and by doing so the Bodhisattvas are themselves helped to rise to Buddhahood, and the Arahats also reach Buddhahood finally. Buddhas are reincarnated solely to help others, since they themselves have already achieved the highest of all levels. They are not reincarnated through any active volition of their own; such an active mental process has no place in Nirvana. They are reincarnated rather by the innate wish to help others through which they have achieved Buddhahood. Their reincarnations occur whenever conditions are suitable, and do not mean that they leave their state in Nirvana. In simile, it is rather as reflections of the moon may be seen on earth in placid lakes and seas when conditions are suitable, while the moon itself remains in its course in the sky. By the same simile, the moon may be reflected in many different places at the same moment, and a Buddha may be incarnate simultaneously in many different bodies. All such incarnate beings, as I have already indicated, can influence, by their own wishes in each life, the place and time when they will be reborn, and after each birth, they have a lingering memory of their previous life which enables others to identify them.

I worked hard at my religious education as a boy, but my life was not all work. I am told that some people in other countries believe the Dalai Lamas were almost prisoners in the Potala Palace. It is true that I could not go out very often because of my studies; but a house was built for my family between the Potala and the city of Lhasa, and I saw them at least every month or six weeks, so that I was not entirely cut off from family life. Indeed, I saw my father very often, for one of the minor daily ceremonies (either in the Potala or the Norbulingka—the summer palace) was the morning tea ceremony, when all the monk officials met for their early bowls of tea—and both my father and I often attended this meeting. Despite our changed circumstances, he still kept up his interest in horses. He would still go out to feed his own horses every morning before he took any food himself, and now that he could afford it, he gave them eggs and tea to strengthen them. And when I was in the summer palace, where the Dalai Lama's stables were situated, and my father came to see me there, I think he often went to call on my horses before he came to call on me.

About a year after we arrived in Lhasa, my elder sister came to join us, and then my eldest brother left the monastery at Kumbum and came to Lhasa too, so that we were all united again. Soon after my elder sister arrived, my younger sister was born, and after her a baby boy. We were all very fond of this baby, and it delighted me to have a younger brother, but to our grief he died when he was only two years old. It was a grief only too familiar to my parents, because so many of their children had already died. But a curious thing happened on the death of the baby. It is the custom in Tibet to consult the lamas and astrologers before a funeral, and sometimes the oracles too. The advice which was given on this occasion was that the body should not be buried but preserved, and he would then be reborn in the same house. As proof, a small mark was to be made on the body with a smear of butter. This was done, and in due course my mother had another baby boy—her last child. And when he was born, the pale mark was seen on the spot of his body where the butter had been smeared. He was the same being, born again in a new body to start his life afresh.

In all these family matters I was able to take some part, but I will agree that most of my time in my boyhood was spent in the company of grown-up men, and there must inevitably be something lacking in a childhood without the constant company of one's mother and other children. However, even if the Potala had been a prison for me, it would have been a spacious and fascinating prison. It is said to be one of the largest buildings in the world. Even after living in it for years, one could never know all its secrets. It entirely covers the top of a hill; it is a city in itself. It was begun by a king of Tibet 1,300 years ago as a pavilion for meditation, and it was greatly enlarged by the Fifth Dalai Lama in the seventeenth century of the Christian era. The central part of the present building, which is thirteen stories high, was built on his orders, but he died when the building had reached the second story. But when he knew that he was dying, he told his Prime Minister to keep his death a secret, because he feared that if it were known that he was dead, the building would be stopped. The Prime Minister found a monk who resembled the Lama and succeeded in concealing the death for thirteen years until the work was finished, but he secretly had a stone carved with a prayer for a reincarnation and had it built into the walls. It can still be seen on the second story today.

This central part of the building contained the great halls for ceremonial occasions, about thirty-five chapels richly carved and painted, four cells for meditation, and the mausoleums of seven Dalai Lamas—some 30 feet high and covered in solid gold and precious stones.

The western wing of the building, which is of later date, housed a community of 175 monks, and in the eastern wing were the government offices, a school for monk officials, and the meeting halls of the National Assembly—the houses of Parliament of Tibet. My own apartments were above the offices, on the top story—400 feet above the town. I had four rooms there. The one which I used most often was about 25 feet square, and its walls were entirely covered by paintings depicting the life of the fifth Dalai Lama, so detailed that the individual portraits were not more than an inch high. When I grew tired of my reading, I often used to sit and follow the story told by this great and elaborate mural which surrounded me.

But apart from its use as office, temple, school, and habitation, the Potala was also an enormous storehouse. Here were rooms full of thousands of priceless scrolls, some a thousand years old. Here were strong rooms filled with the golden regalia of the earliest kings of Tibet, dating back for a thousand years, and the sumptuous gifts they received from the Chinese or Mongol emperors, and the treasures of the Dalai Lamas who succeeded the kings. Here also were stored the armor and armament from the whole of Tibetan history. In the libraries were all the records of Tibetan culture and religion, 7,000 enormous volumes, some of which were said to weigh eighty pounds. Some were written on palm leaves

imported from India a thousand years ago. Two thousand il-
luminated volumes of the scriptures were written in inks
made of powdered gold, silver, iron, copper, conch shell,
turquoise, and coral, each line in a different ink.

Down below the building there were endless underground
storehouses and cellars, containing government stocks of butter, tea, and cloth which were supplied to the monasteries,
the army, and government officials. At the eastern end was
a prison for wrong-doers of high rank—corresponding perhaps to the Tower of London. And on the four corners of
the building were defensive turrets where the Tibetan army
used to keep watch.

In these unique surroundings I pursued my studies and
also pursued my childish interests. I was always fascinated
by mechanical things, but there was nobody who could tell
me anything about them. When I was small, kind people
who knew of this interest sometimes sent me mechanical
toys, such as cars and boats and airplanes. But I was never
content to play with them for long—I always had to take
them to pieces to see how they worked. Usually I managed
to put them together again, though sometimes, as might be
expected, there were disasters. I had a set of Meccano, and
I built cranes and railroad cars with it long before I had ever
seen such things. Later on, I was given an old movie pro-
jector which was operated by turning a handle, and when I
took that to pieces I found the batteries which worked its
electric light. That was my first introduction to electricity,
and I puzzled over the connections all alone until I found
the way to make it go. I had a success, though this was later,
with my wristwatch. I took that entirely to pieces, to study
its principles, and it still worked when I put it together again.

In the Potala, each year began with a ceremony on the
highest roof before sunrise on New Year's Day (a bitterly
cold occasion, when I was not the only one who thought
with longing of the tea ceremony later in the morning) and
religious activities continued day by day throughout the year

until the great Dance of the Lamas the day before New Year's Eve. But in the spring, I myself and my tutors and attendants and some of the government departments moved to the Norbulingka, in a procession which all the people of Lhasa came to see. I was always happy to go to the Norbulingka. The Potala made me proud of our inheritance of culture and craftsmanship, but the Norbulingka was more like a home. It was really a series of small palaces, and chapels, built in a large and beautiful walled garden. Norbulingka means "The Jewel Park." It was started by the Seventh Dalai Lama in the eighteenth century, and successive Dalai Lamas have added their own residences to it ever since. I built one there myself. The founder chose a very fertile spot. In the Norbulingka gardens we grew a radish weighing twenty pounds, and cabbages so large you could not put your arms round them. There were poplars, willows, junipers, and many kinds of flowers and fruit trees: apples, pears, peaches, walnuts, and apricots. We introduced plums and cherry trees while I was there.

There, between my lessons, I could walk and run among the flowers and orchards, and the peacocks and the tame musk deer. There I played on the edge of the lake and twice nearly drowned myself. And there, also in the lake, I used to feed my fish, which would rise to the surface expectantly when they heard my footsteps. I do not know now what has happened to the historical marvels of the Potala. Thinking about them, I sometimes also wonder whether my fish were so unwise as to rise to the surface when they first heard the boots of Chinese soldiers in the Norbulingka. If they did, they have probably been eaten.

One of the minor pleasures of the Norbulingka was that it had a motor generator for electric light, which often broke down, so that I had every excuse to take it to pieces. From that machine, I discovered how internal combustion engines work, and also noticed how the dynamo created a magnetic field when it turned—and I must say that I managed to mend it more often than not.

I tried to make use of this knowledge on three old motor cars, the only ones in Lhasa. There were two 1927 Baby Austins, one blue and the other red and yellow, and a large Dodge of 1931, painted orange. They had been presented to my predecessor and carried over the Himalayas in pieces and then reassembled. However, they had never been used since his death and had stood and been allowed to rust. I longed to make them work. At last I found a young Tibetan who had been trained as a driver in India, and with my eager assistance he managed to put the Dodge in working order, and also one of the Austins, by borrowing parts from the other. These were exciting moments.

I was curious also about the affairs of the world outside Tibet, but naturally much of that curiosity had to go unsatisfied. I had an atlas, and I pored over maps of distant countries and wondered what life was like in them, but I did not know anyone who had ever seen them. I started to teach myself English out of books, because Britain was the only country beyond our immediate neighbors with which we had friendly ties. My tutors read in a Tibetan newspaper, which was published in Kalimpong in India, of the progress of the Second World War, which started in the year I was taken to Lhasa—and they told me about it. Before the end of the war, I was able to read such accounts myself. But few world events affected us in Lhasa. I have sometimes been asked if we followed with interest the attempts of the British to climb Mount Everest. I cannot say that we did. Most Tibetans have to climb too many mountain passes to have any wish to climb higher than they must. And the people of Lhasa, who sometimes climbed for pleasure, chose hills of a reasonable size—and when they came to the top, burned incense, said prayers, and had picnics. That is a pleasure I also enjoy when I have an opportunity.

All in all, it was not an unhappy childhood. The kindness

of my teachers will always remain with me as a memory I shall cherish. They gave me the religious knowledge which has always been and will always be my greatest comfort and inspiration, and they did their best to satisfy what they regarded as a healthy curiosity in other matters. But I know that I grew up with hardly any knowledge of worldly affairs, and it was in that state, when I was sixteen, that I was called upon to lead my country against the invasion of Communist China.

▣ 3 ▣

PEACE OF MIND

Before I tell of the disaster which has overtaken Tibet, I must try to give an impression of the life of our people in our happier days.

Tibet has many neighbors: China, Mongolia, East Turkestan in the east and north, and India, Burma, and the states of Nepal, Sikkim, and Bhutan in the south. Pakistan, Afghanistan, and the Soviet Union are also close to us. For many centuries, we have had relationships with several of these neighbors. With India in particular, we have had strong religious ties during the past thousand years; indeed, our alphabet was derived from Sanskrit, because when Buddhism was brought to Tibet from India there was no Tibetan script, and a script was needed so that religious works could be translated and read by Tibetans. We also had religious and political ties with Mongolia and China. And in earlier times we had connections with Persia and eastern Turkey, so that there is still a resemblance between Persian and Tibetan dress. In more recent history, about the beginning of the twentieth century, we had political relations with Russia, and after that, for a longer period, with Britain.

But despite these neighborly relationships, Tibetans are a distinct and separate race. Our physical appearance and our language and customs are entirely different from those of any of our neighbors. We have no ethnological connection with anyone else in our part of Asia.

Perhaps the best-known quality of Tibet in the recent past was its deliberate isolation. In the world outside, Lhasa was often called the Forbidden City. There were two reasons for this withdrawal from the world. The first, of course, was that the country is naturally isolated. Until the last decade, the route from the borders of India or Nepal to Lhasa was a journey of two months across high Himalayan passes which was blocked for a large part of the year. From my birthplace in the borderland between Tibet and China the journey to Lhasa was even longer, as I have already told—and that borderland itself was over a thousand miles from the sea coast and ports of China.

Isolation was therefore in our blood. We increased our natural isolation by allowing the fewest possible foreigners into our country, simply because we had had experience of strife, especially with China, and had no ambition whatever except to live in peace and pursue our own culture and religion, and we thought that to hold ourselves entirely aloof from the world was the best way of ensuring peace. I must say at once that I think this policy was always a mistake, and my hope and intention is that in the future the gates of Tibet will be kept wide open to welcome visitors from every part of the world.

Tibet has been called the most religious country in the world. I cannot judge if that is so or not, but certainly all normal Tibetans regarded spiritual matters as no less important than material matters, and the most remarkable thing about Tibet was the enormous number of monasteries in it. There are no exact figures, but probably ten per cent of the total population were monks or nuns. This gave a dual nature to the whole of our social system. In fact, it was only in my position as Dalai Lama that lay and monastic authority was combined. I had two prime ministers, one a monk and one a layman, and below them most other offices were duplicated.

The *Khashag* (Cabinet), normally had four members, of whom one was a monk and three were lay officials. Below the Cabinet in rank were two separate offices: the *Yig-tsang* (Secretariat), headed by four monk officials, who were responsible directly to the Dalai Lama and were in charge of religious affairs, and the *Tse-khang* (Finance Office), headed by four laymen, in charge of lay affairs of state.

The departments which any government requires—foreign affairs, agriculture, taxation, posts and telegraphs, defense, the army, etc.—were each under two or three chairmen. There were also two chief justices, and the city courts had two judges. Finally, several of the provinces of Tibet had two governors.

The National Assembly could be convened in three forms. Its smallest form, which was almost continuously in session, included the eight officials of the *Yig-tsang* and *Tse-khang,* together with other high lay officials and representatives of the three great monasteries near Lhasa—about twenty representatives in all. This nucleus assembly could convene a larger body of about thirty members to consider specific problems, and on matters of great importance, such as the confirmation of the discovery of the new reincarnation of the Dalai Lama, a full assembly of about 400 members from all the official and non-official levels were called into session.

Outside the monasteries, our social system was feudal. There was inequality of wealth between the landed aristocracy at one extreme and the poorest peasants at the other. It was difficult to move up into the class of aristocracy, but not impossible. For example, a soldier could be awarded a title and land for bravery, and both were hereditary.

But on the other hand, promotion to higher ranks in the monasteries and among officials was democratic. A boy could enter a monastery from any social class, and his progress there would depend on his own ability. And indeed it might also be said that the reincarnation of high lamas had a democratic influence, because incarnate lamas often chose to be reborn in humble families, as the Thirteenth Dalai Lama did, so that men from lowly surroundings, like myself, were found in the highest positions in the monastic world.

(I use the past tense, reluctantly, because Tibet is under attack and one cannot say at this moment which of our institutions still exist and which are being destroyed.)

The monasteries had their own monk craftsmen to provide their own needs, and they traded to some extent. Some of them had large grants of land, and some had endowments which they invested, but others had neither of these possessions. They often received personal gifts. Some acted as moneylenders, and a few charged rates of interest higher than I can approve. But on the whole they were not economically self-sufficient. Most of them depended more or less on subsidies, mainly of food, from the government. This was the reason why the government held stocks of grain and tea and butter, and also of cloth, in the cellars of the Potala and elsewhere. These subsidies, of course, came ultimately from the rents or taxes of the laity.

I have mentioned soldiers. We had an army, but it was very small. Its main work was to man the frontier posts and to stop unauthorized foreigners coming into the country. This army also formed our police force, except in the city of Lhasa, which had its own police, and in the monasteries. In Lhasa, the army added military color to ceremonies and lined the route whenever I left the palaces. It had a curious history. About fifty years ago, when we were having trouble with the Chinese, my predecessor decided to bring the army up to date by employing a few foreign instructors for a short while. Nobody could tell which was the best foreign army to model it on, so he had one regiment trained by Russians, one by Japanese, and one by British. The British system turned out to be the most suitable, so the whole army was organized on British lines. The British instructors left Tibet more than a generation ago, but up till 1949 the army still used British words of command in its drill, since there had been no such martial words in our language, and among the Tibetan marches played by its military bands were the melodies of "It's a Long Way to Tipperary," "Auld Lang Syne," and "God Save the King." But the words of these tunes, if any Tibetan ever knew them, were forgotten long ago. However, I do not want to give the impression that our army was anachronistic or absurd; it was not. It had never been brought up to date by being mechanized, because that was impossible. It was far too small to defend our large country against attack, but for its own limited purposes it was quite effective, and its men were brave.

I think everyone who is interested in Tibet has been able to read about life in Lhasa, because most of the foreign travelers who have visited Tibet have made Lhasa their objective and have written books about it, so I need not dwell upon it. They have described the almost continuous round of celebrations and ceremonies from one year's end to the next, and the elaborate parties given by the richer people, their beautiful and decorative dress, the holy walks around the ring road called Ling-kor, and the picnics by the river in the summer which were perhaps the most popular pastime of all. Indeed, the travelers may have been able to describe these affairs in greater detail than I could offer from my own experience, because of course I did not share in many of them myself. Whenever I took part in ceremonies, I naturally became the focal point of them, and the essence of those ceremonies was the reverence which the people showed to me. Therefore, whenever I watched ceremonies in which I had no part, such as religious dances in the Potala or dramatic performances in the Norbulingka gardens, I watched from behind gauze curtains so that I could see without being seen. But I would like to add one general comment to the travelers' tales. We Tibetans love a show or a ceremony, whether it be religious or secular, and we love all ceremonial and elegant dress, and—which is perhaps even more important as a national characteristic—we love a joke. I do not know if we always laugh at the same things as Westerners, but we can almost always find something to laugh about. We are what Westerners call "easygoing" and happy-go-lucky by nature, and it is only in the most desperate circumstances that our sense of humor fails us.

But Lhasa was the only place where social life was so elaborate. Outside the city and a few other towns and the monasteries, the material life of the people was very much like the life of a peasant class elsewhere, except in the degree of its isolation. The distances were vast, and there was no communication whatever except by mail-runners on foot and on horseback. In the mountains, the climate is very harsh and most of the soil is poor, so that the population was sparse and life was solitary and extremely simple. Most people in the distant marches of Tibet had never been to Lhasa, or even perhaps met anyone else who had been there. From year to year they tilled the earth and bred their yaks and other animals, and neither heard nor saw what happened in the world beyond their own horizon. I believe there are many such people, not only in Tibet but in all the poorer countries in the world, whatever their system of government.

I do not pretend that every single Tibetan was a gentle and kindly person—of course we had our criminals and sinners. To mention a single example, we had many nomads, and though most of them were peaceful, some of their clans were not above brigandage. Consequently, settled people in certain neighborhoods had to take care to arm themselves, and travelers in such places preferred to go in large companies for protection. The people who lived in the eastern district where I was born, including the Khampas, were law-abiding on the whole, but they were the kind of people to whom a rifle is almost more important than any other possession, as a symbol of manly independence.

Yet the sense of religion pervaded even the wildest places, and most of the wildest hearts, and one would often see its symbol, too, in the poorest tents of nomads: the altar with the butter lamp before it.

During my education, I learned very little of any other social system but our own; and Tibetans in general, I think, regarded it as the natural state of affairs and never gave a thought to any theories of government. But as I grew up, I began to see how much was wrong with it. Our inequality in the distribution of wealth was certainly not in accordance with Buddhist teaching, and in the few years when I held effective power in Tibet, I managed to make some fundamental reforms. I appointed a Reforms Committee of fifty members, lay and monk officials and representatives of the monasteries, and a smaller standing committee to examine all the reforms that were needed and report to the larger body, and thence to me.

The simplest reform was in the collection of taxes. The amount of revenue required from each district had always been fixed by the government, but from time immemorial it had been understood that the district authorities could collect as much extra as they liked, or as much as they were able, to pay their own expenses and salaries. As this was permitted by law, the people had to pay up, and I was not very old when I saw what a temptation it was toward injustice. So I changed the whole system, in consultation with both the Cabinet and the Reforms Committee. The district authorities had to collect the exact amount required and remit it all to the Treasury, and they were paid a fixed salary by the government. This pleased everyone, except some district authorities who had been making more money than they should.

Even more fundamental reforms were needed in our system of land tenure. The whole land of Tibet was the property of the State, and most peasant farmers held their land under a kind of leasehold directly from the State. Some of them paid their rent in kind, with a proportion of their produce, and this was the main source of the government's stocks which were distributed to the monasteries, the army, and officials. Some paid by labor, and some had always been required to provide free transport for government officials, and in some cases for the monasteries too. My predecessor, the Thirteenth Dalai Lama, had abolished the system of free transport, because it had become an unfair burden, and he had fixed charges for the use of horses, mules, and yaks. But since then, prices had risen, the fixed charges had become inadequate, and the right to demand transport had been given to far too many people. So I ordered that in future no transport should be demanded without the special sanction of the Cabinet, and I increased the rates to be paid for it.

It may be misleading to say that these peasants were tenants. It was a mere concept that the land belonged to the State. A peasant's land was heritable, and he could lease it to others, mortgage it, or even sell his right to it—though the right to land was rarely sold because a peasant's first duty was always to hand on the land intact to the next generation. He could only be dispossessed if he failed to pay his dues of produce or labor, which were not excessive. So in practice he had all the rights of a freeholder, and his dues to the State were really a land tax paid in kind, rather than a rent.

For many years, the government had been making loans to these peasants whenever times were bad. I found that no effort had been made to reclaim the loans or the interest, and the amount outstanding had become so enormous that clearly the peasants would never be able to repay it. My

Committee made a detailed investigation, and we decided to divide the peasants into three categories. Those who could not either pay the accumulated interest or repay the capital were freed from the debt altogether. Some could not pay the interest out of their annual earnings, but had saved up enough to repay the capital, and these were told to repay it in installments. But some had become quite wealthy since they received the loans, and they had to pay both interest and capital in installments. These measures were welcomed by the peasants. Most of them had been worried by the debt which was hanging over their heads, and they were glad to know where they stood.

But the most urgent single reform which our social system needed was in the large private estates. These estates had been granted long ago to aristocratic families. They were hereditary, and in return for the grant each family had to provide one male heir in each generation to be trained and to work as a government official. Some families also made a payment to the State. The remainder of the estate's income provided the official's salary. This was how the lay officials were recruited. On these estates, peasants worked on behalf of the aristocracy in conditions over which the government had no direct control, and the landlords exercised a feudal right of justice, which they often had to delegate to their stewards, for most of them had to spend most of the year in Lhasa to carry out their duties to the State.

My Committee and Cabinet examined the whole of this ancient arrangement, and when I received their recommendations I decided that the greater part of all these large estates should revert to State ownership on payment of compensation to the families to which they had been granted, and that the officials should be paid their salaries in cash. The land should then be distributed among the peasants who already worked it. So all peasants would have been put on an equal basis as tenants of the State, and the administration of justice would have been unified. A similar reform was certainly needed on the large estates which had been granted to monasteries, but we decided to start with the privately owned estates.

However, before we reached this stage of our reforms, the Chinese were in command of us, and we could not carry through such a far-reaching change without their agreement. But they had come with their own Communist ideas of land reform, which the Tibetan peasants disliked very much, and if our government had put through this popular reform, the Chinese reforms would have been even more unpopular than they were. So, however hard we pressed them, they would never either say yes or no to this proposal. And finally, more drastic events overtook us, and for the present it had to be abandoned.

So we had made a beginning in changing our social system from the medieval to the modern, before our progress was stopped by events which we could not control. There was still much to be done to improve the lot of the ordinary people of Tibet, and I shall write in another chapter of what I and my government hope to do in the future. Yet with all the faults of its system, and the rigor of its climate, I am sure that Tibet was among the happiest of lands. The system certainly gave opportunities for oppression, but Tibetans on the whole are not oppressive people. There was very little of the cruelty of man to man which used to arise in the past from feudal systems, for in every class, and in all vicissitudes, religion was both a controlling influence and a constant comfort and support.

It is often said by people of other religions that belief in rebirth—the law of Karma—tends to make people accept inequalities of fortune—perhaps accept them too readily. This is only partly true. A poor Tibetan peasant was less inclined to envy or resent his rich Tibetan landlord, because he knew that each of them was reaping the seed he had sown in his previous life. But on the other hand, there is nothing whatever in the law of Karma to discourage a man from trying to improve his own lot in his present life. And of course our religion encourages every attempt to improve the lot of others. All true charity has a double benefit—to the receiver in his present life, and to the giver in his present life or in his life to come. In this light, Tibetans accepted our social system without any question.

And feudal though the system was, it was different from any other feudal system, because at the apex of it was the incarnation of Chenresi, a being whom all the people, for hundreds of years, had regarded with the highest reverence. The people felt that above all the petty officials of state, there was a final appeal to a source of justice which they could absolutely trust; and in fact, no ruler with the traditions and training and religious grace of a Dalai Lama could possibly have become an unjust tyrant.

So we were happy. Desire brings discontent; happiness springs from a peaceful mind. For many Tibetans, material life was hard, but they were not the victims of desire; and in simplicity and poverty among our mountains, perhaps there was more peace of mind than there is in most of the cities of the world.

▣ 4 ▣

OUR NEIGHBOR CHINA

During the few years of my active rule in Tibet, our legal status as a nation, which had never worried us before, suddenly became tremendously important to us. At this point, therefore, I want to give a factual history of our position in the world.

In prehistoric times Tibet is supposed to have been an inland sea surrounded by forests and snow mountains which no human beings claimed. When humans appeared there, some of them gained recognition by the rest as chiefs, and these chiefs guided the life of their tribes.

The amalgamation of these tribes as a single Tibet nation, with Nya-Tri-Tsenpo as the first king, was achieved no less than 2,000 years ago, in the Wood Tiger Year, corresponding to 127 B.C., or 418 years (according to the Indian manner of reckoning) after the death of Lord Buddha. He was succeeded by forty generations of kings. During the reigns of the first twenty-seven, the religion called Bön flourished in the country, together with many strange beliefs.

It was during the reign of the twenty-eighth king, whose name was Lha-Tho-Ri-Nyen-Tsen, that the next most significant event in the history of Tibet occurred. A volume of Lord Buddha's teachings fell into his hands, and the spread of Buddhism in Tibet began.

The thirty-third king, Song-Tsen-Gampo, did much to establish the new religion more firmly. He was born in the Earth Bull Year (629 A.D., 1,173 years after the death of Lord Buddha), and while he was young he sent his minister, Thumi-Sam-Bhota, to study in India. After his return to Tibet, the minister drafted the present Tibetan alphabet. The king established the noble customs of spiritual and material life, and formulated ten rules for religious services and sixteen rules for public conduct. Temples, including the Jokhang in Lhasa, were built in his reign, and many chapels, and the building of the Potala was begun. Besides having three Tibetan wives, the king married both a Chinese and a Nepalese princess, and perhaps at their instigation, two images of Lord Buddha were brought from Nepal and from China. It was before one of these images, in the Jokhang, that I bowed when I first reached Lhasa at the age of four. During King Song-Tsen-Gampo's reign, skill in many trades was learned from India, China, and Nepal, so that the economy of Tibet was improved, the people became more prosperous and happy, and the nation increased in power.

In the reign of the thirty-sixth king, Tri-Dhi-Tsuk-Ten, there was a period of war between the Chinese and Tibetans, and the king's minister Ta-Ra-Lu-Gong conquered several Chinese provinces. To this day a stone pillar stands in front of the Potala commemorating the victories of this minister.

The thirty-seventh king, Thi-Song-Deu-Tsen, was born in the Iron Horse Year (790 A.D., 1,334 years after the death of Lord Buddha). During his reign, he invited the learned Indian scholars Khenchen-Bodi-Sattawa and Lopon-Pema-Samba to come to Tibet. Many Indian pandits, and Tibetans who understood Sanskrit, worked to translate the teachings of Lord Buddha into the Tibetan language. At this time, the Samye Monastery was established, and the first seven monks were ordained in Tibet. The country's political power also increased, so that territories under Tibet were spread far and wide.

By the reign of the fortieth king, Nga-Dak-Tri-Ral, who was born in the Fire Dog Year (866 A.D., 1,410 years from the death of Lord Buddha), the number of monks in Tibet had increased enormously. There was another war between Tibet and China during his reign, and again the Tibetans conquered large parts of China, but Tibetan lamas and the Chinese monks known as Hashangs acted as mediators to bring peace. In the Sino-Tibetan border area called Khung-Khu-Meru, the frontier was marked by a stone pillar, and similar pillars were erected in front of the palace of the Chinese emperor and in front of the Jokhang in Lhasa. On these three pillars a mutual pledge was inscribed, in Chinese and Tibetan characters, that neither Tibet nor China should trespass beyond the marked frontier.

These three kings, the thirty-third, thirty-seventh, and fortieth, are regarded as the greatest in the history of Tibet, and our people honor them to this day.

However, in the Iron Bird Year (901 A.D., 1,445 years from the death of Lord Buddha), the forty-first king, whose name was Lang-Dar-Ma, came to the throne, and his reign was marked by his undoing of everything his predecessors had done. He and his ministers did their best to destroy the Buddhist religion and the customs of Tibet. After an evil reign of six years, he was assassinated.

Thus, just over a thousand years had elapsed from the reign of the first king of Tibet till the death of the forty-first, and during those first thousand years the country had steadily grown in material and spiritual strength. But after the death of Lang-Dar-Ma, the kingdom disintegrated. The King had had two queens, and two sons, one of whom was not his real son. The queens quarreled, the ministers took sides, and finally Tibet was divided between the two princes. This division led to further sub-divisions, and Tibet became a land of many tiny kingdoms. So it remained 347 years.

But in the thirteenth century of the Christian calendar, the high lama of the great Sakya monastery, whose name was Chogyal-Phag-Pa, went to China to become the religious instructor of the Chinese emperor, Sechen. And in the Water Bull Year (1253 A.D., 1,797 years from the death of Lord Buddha) he returned and became the ruler of all the three *Cholkhas* or provinces of Tibet—the first of the priest-kings of our country. For the next ninety-six years, this country was ruled by a succession of twenty lamas of Sakya, and after that, for eighty-six years—from 1349 to 1435 A.D.— by a succession of eleven lamas of Phamo Drupa lineage. Then there was a return to a secular monarchy. Four generations of Rirpong kings ruled from 1435 to 1565, and three Tsangpa kings from 1566 to 1641. It was then in the Water Horse Year (1642 A.D., 2,186 years from the death of Lord Buddha) that a Dalai Lama received temporal power over the whole of the country, and the present form of Tibetan government known as *Gaden-Phodrang* was founded. Since then, for over 300 years, ten successive Dalai Lamas have been the spiritual and temporal rulers of Tibet, and during their absence or minority lay and monk regents have carried on the government in their name.

It was the Fifth Dalai Lama who first assumed these temporal powers. The First Dalai Lama had been a disciple of the founder of the Gelukpa sect, Tsongkhapa, and both these incarnations were exceptionally learned men, the first in spiritual matters, and the fifth in both spiritual and temporal matters. In 1652 A.D., the first Manchu emperor of China, Shun-Tse, invited the Fifth Dalai Lama, whom he regarded as his religious instructor, to visit China, and received him there with homage as King of Tibet.

For two and a half centuries of the rule of the Dalai Lamas, until about the end of the nineteenth Christian century, there was a reciprocal personal relationship between the Dalai Lamas and the Emperors of China; a relationship of religious leadership on one side and a rather tenuous secular leadership on the other. The Emperor appointed two officials called Ambans to represent him in Lhasa. They exercised some authority, but they exercised it through the government of the Dalai Lama, and in the course of time their authority gradually declined.

It was during the reign of my great predecessor, the Thirteenth Dalai Lama, that Tibet first began to expand its international relations. I have already told how the Thirteenth Dalai Lama improved the living standards of our people, and how he reorganized our army. He also sent students abroad to study; established small hydroelectric plants and industries; introduced postal and telegraph services; issued stamps, new gold and silver coins, and currency notes. He also made changes in the curriculum of religious studies in Gelukpa monasteries. And during his reign Tibet made a number of international agreements.

Toward the end of the nineteenth century, the British government of India began to want to establish trade with Tibet, and various minor border disputes had also arisen between Tibetan and British territory in the Himalayas. The British had to decide whether to negotiate these matters with Tibet itself or with China. Except for a single document in 1247 no treaty had been signed between Tibet and China since the stone pillars had been inscribed in the year 822, so there was not much to guide the British choice. However, in 1893 they signed a convention with China which fixed the boundary and gave the British certain trading rights in the south of Tibet.

But the Tibetan government simply disregarded this convention. When boundary marks were erected by British and Chinese commissioners, the Tibetans waited till they had gone and then took the marks away again, and when the British applied for their trade concessions, the government told them the convention had only been signed by China and had no force whatever in Tibet. The Tibetans, in their easy-going nature, had had the Chinese Ambans living with them for generations. But this was the first time that any other power had wanted to make a formal international agreement with Tibet, and it had never occurred to Tibetans that the mere presence of the Ambans in Lhasa might give the Chinese government an opportunity to claim a right to sign agreements on Tibet's behalf. Nor had they thought until then that the Chinese wished to deprive them of their independence.

The British became increasingly irritated at not receiving their trading rights, and no doubt also at losing their boundary marks. Lord Curzon, the British Viceroy of India, said he regarded "Chinese suzerainty over Tibet as a constitutional fiction—a political affectation which has only been maintained because of its convenience to both parties." In 1903, he sent a military force to Lhasa. It halted for a long time on the way, and while it was halted, the Amban sent a message to the British commander to say that he would come to meet him. But the Tibetan government would not allow the Amban to leave Lhasa. The Tibetan army fought the British troops and were beaten, the Dalai Lama fled towards the east, and the British advanced to Lhasa in 1904 and signed a convention with the Tibetan government.

In the Dalai Lama's absence, the convention was signed by the Regent, using the Dalai Lama's seal, and also sealed by the Cabinet, the National Assembly, and the monasteries of Drepung, Sera, and Gaden. Tibet in fact, had made a formal international agreement as a sovereign power. It confirmed the boundary and trading rights, and among other things, it undertook that no foreign power should be allowed to intervene in Tibetan affairs without the consent of the British government. China was not mentioned at all in the document, and by this omission it must have been included among the other unspecified foreign powers. As soon as the convention was signed, the British forces marched out of Tibet and never threatened us again.

The Chinese government never raised any objection to this treaty. Two years later, in 1906, the British seem to have had some fear that the Chinese might interfere with their trading concessions, and they made an agreement in which the Chinese government formally accepted the Anglo-Tibetan treaty. So the remnant of Chinese power in Tibet was acknowledged to have ended, so far as international agreements had any worth.

However, the British were inconsistent. This was a period when Russia and Britain were rivals for "spheres of influence" in Asia, and in 1907 they signed an agreement in which they both undertook not to interfere with Tibet, and only to negotiate with Tibet through China as an intermediary. This agreement, in contradiction to the others, and in spite of Britain's experience that China had no practical authority in our country, recognized that China had suzerainty over Tibet.

Suzerainty is a vague and ancient term. Perhaps it was the nearest western political term to describe the relations between Tibet and China from 1720 to 1890, but still, it was very inaccurate, and the use of it has misled whole generations of western statesmen. It did not take into account the reciprocal spiritual relationship, or recognize that the relationship was a personal matter between the Dalai Lamas and the Manchu emperors. There are many such ancient eastern relationships which cannot be described in ready-made western political terms.

One explanation of the British inconsistency is that they had already secured for themselves a favorable position in Tibet which was not affected by the new agreement, and were willing to give up their right to deal directly with Tibet in order to prevent Russia from doing the same. But another explanation is that the first two treaties were made by the British government in India, and the third by the British government in London, and that one did not really understand what the other was doing. The typically eastern relationship of China and Tibet may well have been better understood in India than in England. But at all events, neither Tibet nor China had been asked to sign this new agreement, and so it did not bind Tibet in the least to recognize China's suzerainty.

One unfortunate effect of the British expedition to Lhasa was that it aroused the Chinese to the fact that their own power had disappeared, so that when the British withdrew, after severely mauling the Tibetan army, they left Tibet with very little defense against anything the Chinese might decide to do. And the Russian agreement had the added effect of giving the Chinese a free hand in Tibet while it tied the British to non-intervention. So China, in spite of her own agreement with Britain, invaded Tibet. The Dalai Lama was forced to flee again, this time to British protection in India, and the Chinese army reached Lhasa in 1910.

But the Manchu dynasty was tottering. In 1911, revolution broke out in China. The pay and supplies of the Chinese troops in Tibet were cut off, they revolted against their officers, and in 1912 the Tibetans drove the remnants of them, together with the Ambans, out of the country. With that Tibet became completely independent, and from 1912 until the Chinese invasion in 1950, neither the Chinese nor any other state had any power whatever in Tibet.

During the expulsion of the Chinese army, the Dalai Lama returned from India, and he issued declarations that Tibet was an independent nation. On these declarations a seal which had been presented to the Dalai Lamas by the Tibetan people was used instead of a seal which the Chinese had presented to them long before. Some ancient Tibetan documents had been headed with the words: *By order of the Emperor of China, the Dalai Lama is the Pontiff of Buddhism.* But the Thirteenth Dalai Lama changed the heading to read: *By order of Lord Buddha. . . .*

But having achieved and declared our independence, and

being weary of such struggles, we retired into our ancient solitude. We made no treaty with China, and consequently our *de facto* independence was not given a legal international form. In 1913, the British tried to settle the matter by inviting Chinese and Tibetan representatives to a conference at Simla in India. The three representatives met on equal terms, and after a very long discussion they initialed a draft convention. In this, the British persuaded the Tibetans to agree to their concept of Chinese suzerainty, and persuaded the Chinese to agree to the autonomy of Tibet. Britain and China were to respect the territorial integrity of Tibet, not to send troops into Tibet, and not to interfere with the administration of the Tibetan government.

But although the Chinese representative had initialed this agreement, the Chinese government refused to sign it, and so Tibet and Britain signed alone, with a separate declaration that China was debarred from any privileges under the agreement so long as she refused to sign it. She never signed it, and so never claimed suzerainty in this legal form.

So matters remained. The Chinese government went on insisting, whenever the question arose, that Tibet was part of China, but meanwhile, there were no Chinese with any authority whatever in Tibet, and for thirty-eight years Tibet pursued her own independent way. Tibet took no part in the Sino-Japanese War, and even in the Second World War she insisted on her neutrality, and refused to allow the transport of war material from India to China through Tibetan territory. Throughout this period Tibetans never took any active steps to prove their independence to the outside world, because it never seemed to be necessary. But from time to time, other governments acted in a way which proved that they accepted it. Thus in 1947, when a conference of all Asian countries was held in Delhi, the Tibetan delegation attended on an equal footing with the rest, and the Tibetan flag flew among the flags of the other nations. In the same year, after India had become independent, her government replied to a Tibetan message in these words: "The government of India would be glad to have an assurance that it is the intention of the Tibetan government to continue relations on the existing basis until new agreements are reached on matters that either party may wish to take up. This is the procedure adopted by all other countries with which India has inherited treaty relations from His Majesty's government." In 1948, a trade delegation from the government of Tibet visited India, China, France, Italy, the United Kingdom and the United States of America, and the passports which the Tibetan government had issued to the delegates were accepted by the governments of all these countries.

For the first twenty-two years of our independence, there were no Chinese officials of any kind in Tibet, but in 1934, after the death of the Thirteenth Dalai Lama, a Chinese delegation came to Lhasa to present religious offerings. After presenting the offerings, the delegation remained in Lhasa on the grounds that it wanted to complete some talks on the Sino-Tibetan border which had been left unfinished. However, the position of these Chinese was exactly the same as those of the Nepalese and British, and later the Indian Missions which were also in Lhasa—and in 1949 even these remaining Chinese were expelled from the country.

So one may sum up this brief history by saying that Tibet is a distinct and ancient nation, which for many centuries enjoyed a relationship of mutual respect with China. It is true that there were times when China was strong and Tibet was weak, and China invaded Tibet. Similarly, looking farther back into history, there were times when Tibet invaded China. There is no basis whatever in history for the Chinese claim that Tibet was part of China. From 1912 until the fateful year of 1950, Tibet enjoyed complete *de facto* independence of any other nation, and our legal status is now exactly the same as it was in 1912. That status has been analyzed in the utmost detail in recent years by the International Commission of Jurists, and rather than express my own opinion of it, I will quote the conclusion which that body of distinguished and impartial experts submitted to the United Nations and published in their report on *The Question of Tibet and the Rule of Law* in 1959:

> Tibet's position on the expulsion of the Chinese in 1912 can fairly be described as one of *de facto* independence and there are, as explained, strong legal grounds for thinking that any form of legal subservience to China had vanished. It is therefore submitted that the events of 1911–12 mark the reemergence of Tibet as a fully sovereign state, independent in fact and in law of Chinese control.

▣ 5 ▣

INVASION

In 1948, while I was still a student, the government heard there were Chinese Communist spies in the country. They had come to find out how strong our army was, and whether we were receiving military aid from any foreign power.

They cannot have found it very hard to discover the facts they wanted. Far from receiving military aid, we had only six Europeans in Tibet, so far as I was aware. Three of them, one missionary and two radio operators, were British. The other three were two Austrians and one White Russian, all of whom had been refugees from British internment camps in India during the war. None of them had anything to do with military matters.

As for the army, its strength was 8,500 officers and men. There were more than enough rifles for them, but only about fifty pieces of artillery of various kinds—250 mortars and about 200 machine guns. The purpose of the army, as I have said, was to stop unauthorized travelers and act as a police force. It was quite inadequate to fight a war.

Soon after this first sign of impending trouble, more serious news was heard from the eastern parts of Tibet. The governor of eastern Tibet, whose name was Lhalu, was stationed in the town of Chamdo, close to the frontier, and he had one of the British radio operators with him, the other being in Lhasa. Soon coded signals began to come in from the governor reporting that the Chinese were moving up strong forces and massing them along our eastern border. It was obvious that they intended either to attack or intimidate us.

As soon as this alarming information reached the Cabinet, they convened a meeting of the National Assembly. Evidently, Tibet was facing a far more serious threat from the east than it had ever faced in all the centuries before. Communism had conquered China, and given the country a military strength it had not had for many generations. So the threat to us was not only more powerful, it was also different in its very nature. In past centuries, there had always been some religious sympathy between our countries, but now we were threatened not only with military domination, but also with the domination of an alien materialistic creed which, so far as any of us understood it in Tibet, seemed totally abhorrent.

The Assembly agreed unanimously that Tibet had neither the material resources nor the arms or men to defend its integrity against a serious attack, and so they decided to make an urgent appeal to other countries, in the hope of persuading the Chinese to halt before it was too late. Four delegations were appointed to visit Britain, the United States of America, India, and Nepal to ask for help. Before the delegations left Lhasa, telegrams were sent to these four governments, to tell them of the apparent threat to our independence, and of our government's wish to send the delegations.

The replies to these telegrams were terribly disheartening. The British government expressed their deepest sympathy for the people of Tibet, and regretted that owing to Tibet's geographical position, since India had been granted independence, they could not offer help. The government of the United States also replied in the same sense and declined to receive our delegation. The Indian government also made it clear that they would not give us military help, and advised us not to offer any armed resistance, but to open negotiations for a peaceful settlement on the basis of the Simla agreement of 1914. So we learned that in military matters we were alone.

It happened that Lhalu's term as governor of eastern Tibet was over, and at this crucial moment he had to be replaced by another official, Ngabo Ngawang Jigme. Ngabo left Lhasa for the eastern province, and as the situation was so delicate the Cabinet told Lhalu to stay at his post to help his successor, sharing the responsibility with him. But Ngabo soon said he was ready to take the full responsibility, and so Lhalu was recalled. Very soon afterwards, without any formal warning, the armies of Communist China invaded Tibet.

For a short time, and in a few places, the Tibetan army fought them back with some success, aided by volunteers from the local race of Khampas. But our army was hopelessly outnumbered and outmatched. The change of governor had confused the administration, and Ngabo began to move his headquarters back from Chamdo toward the west. When the Tibetan troops, retreating from the frontier, arrived at Chamdo, they found he had already abandoned the place, and so they had to burn the armory and ammunition store and join him in further retreat.

But retreat was of no avail. Ngabo found his line of communication cut, and himself outflanked by more mobile Chinese forces, and he and many Tibetan troops were forced to surrender.

The Chamdo radio transmitter and its British operator were also captured, and so for a time no news of what was hap-

pening reached the government. And then two officials arrived in Lhasa, sent by Ngabo with the Chinese commander's permission, to tell the Cabinet that he was a prisoner,
to ask for authority to negotiate terms of peace, and also to
give the Cabinet an assurance from the Chinese commander
that China would not extend her rule over more Tibetan
territory.

While these disasters were taking place in the distant eastern marches of Tibet, the government in Lhasa was consulting the oracles and the high lamas, and guided by their
advice, the Cabinet came to see me with the solemn request
that I should take over the responsibility of government.

This filled me with anxiety. I was only sixteen. I was far
from having finished my religious education. I knew nothing about the world and had no experience of politics, and
yet I was old enough to know how ignorant I was and how
much I had still to learn. I protested at first that I was too
young, for eighteen was the accepted age for a Dalai Lama
to take over active control from his Regent. Yet I understood very well why the oracles and lamas had caused the
request to be made. The long years of Regency after the
death of each Dalai Lama were an inevitable weakness in
our system of government. During my own minority, there
had been dissensions between separate factions in our government, and the administration of the country had deterio-
rated. We had reached a state in which most people were
anxious to avoid responsibility, rather than accept it. Yet
now, under the threat of invasion, we were more in need of
unity than ever before, and I, as Dalai Lama, was the only
person whom everybody in the country would unanimously
follow.

I hesitated—but then the National Assembly met, and
added its plea to the Cabinet's, and I saw that at such a serious moment in our history, I could not refuse my responsibilities. I had to shoulder them, put my boyhood behind
me, and immediately prepare myself to lead my country, as

well as I was able, against the vast power of Communist China.

So I accepted, with trepidation, and full powers were conferred on me with traditional celebration. In my name a general amnesty was proclaimed, and every convict in prison in Tibet was given freedom.

At just about that time, my eldest brother arrived in Lhasa from the east. He had returned, as Abbot, to the monastery of Kumbum, near the village where we had been born. In this Chinese-controlled territory, while he was Abbot, he had been witness to the downfall of the governor under Chiang Kai-shek's regime, and the advance of the armies of the new Communist government. He had seen a year of confusion, oppression and terror, in which the Chinese Communists had claimed that they had come to protect the people, and had promised them freedom to pursue their own religion, and yet at the same time had begun a systematic undermining and destruction of religious life. He himself had been kept under a strict guard and subjected to an almost continuous course of Communist argument, until finally, the Chinese had explained to him that they intended to reclaim the whole of Tibet, which they still insisted was a part of China, and to convert it all to communism. Then they tried to persuade him to go to Lhasa as their emissary, and to persuade me and my government to agree to their domination. They promised to make him governor of Tibet if he succeeded. Of course, he refused to do anything of the kind. But at last he saw that his life would be in danger if he continued to refuse, and he also saw that he had a duty to warn me of the Chinese plans. So he pretended to agree, and thus managed to escape from Chinese supervision and reached Lhasa with a detailed warning of the dangers we were facing.

By then, the Cabinet had taken steps to put our case before the United Nations. While we were waiting for it to be considered, it seemed to me that the first of my duties must be to follow the advice of the Indian government, and try to reach an agreement with the Chinese before more harm was done. So I wrote to the Chinese government, through the commander of the army which was occupying Chamdo. I said that during my minority relations had been strained between our countries, but that now I had taken over full responsibility and sincerely wanted to restore the friendship which had existed in the past. I pleaded with them to return the Tibetans who had been captured by their army, and to withdraw from the part of Tibet which they had occupied by force.

At about the same time, my Cabinet convened the National Assembly again, in order to test public opinion about the threat which confronted us. One result of this Assembly was very unwelcome in my eyes. The members pointed out that the Chinese armies might advance to Lhasa and capture it at any moment, and they decided that I should be requested to leave the city and go to the town of Yatung, near the border of India, so that I would be out of any personal danger. I did not want to go at all. I wanted to stay where I was and do what I could to help my people. But the Cabinet also urged me to go, and in the end I had to give in. This conflict was often to occur again, as I shall tell. As a young and able-bodied man, my instinct was to share whatever risks my people were undergoing, but to Tibetans, the person of the Dalai Lama is supremely precious, and whenever the conflict arose I had to allow my people to take far more care of me than I would have thought of taking of myself.

So I prepared to go. Before I left, I appointed two Prime Ministers—a high monk official called Losang Tashi, and a veteran and experienced lay administrator called Lukhangwa. I gave them full authority and made them jointly responsible, and told them they need only refer to me in matters of the very highest importance.

It was in the minds of my ministers then that if the worst came to the worst I might have to go to India for refuge, as my predecessor had done when the Chinese invaded us forty years before. I was advised to send a small part of my treasure there. So some gold dust and bars of silver were taken from Lhasa and put in a vault across the border in Sikkim, and there they lay for the next nine years. In the end, we needed them badly.

The next grievous blow to us was the news that the General Assembly of the United Nations had decided not to consider the question of Tibet. This filled us with consternation. We had put our faith in the United Nations as a source of justice, and we were astonished to hear that it was on British initiative that the question had been shelved. We had had very friendly relations with the British for a long time, and had benefited greatly from the wisdom and experience of many distinguished servants of the British Crown; and it was Britain who had implied her recognition of our independence by concluding treaties with us as a sovereign power. Yet now, the British representative said the legal position of Tibet was not very clear, and he seemed to suggest that even now, after thirty-eight years without any Chinese in our country, we might still be legally subject to China's suzerainty. The attitude of the Indian representative was equally disappointing. He said he was certain a peaceful settlement could be made and Tibet's autonomy could be safeguarded, and that the best way to ensure this was to abandon the idea of discussing the matter in the General Assembly.

This was a worse disappointment than the earlier news that nobody would offer us any military help. Now our friends would not even help us to present our plea for justice. We felt abandoned to the hordes of the Chinese army.

Of course, looking back at our history now, it is easy to see how our own policies had helped to put us in this desperate position. When we won our complete independence, in 1912, we were quite content to retire into isolation. It never occurred to us that our independence, so obvious a fact to us, needed any legal proof to the outside world. If only we had applied to join the League of Nations or the United Nations, or even appointed ambassadors to a few of the leading powers, before our crisis came, I am sure these signs of sovereignty would have been accepted without any question, and the plain justice of our cause would not have been clouded, as it was, by subtle legal discussions based on ancient treaties which had been made under quite different circumstances. Now we had to learn the bitter lesson that the world has grown too small for any people to live in harmless isolation.

The only thing we could do was pursue our negotiations as best we could. We decided to give Ngabo the authority he had requested. One of the two officials he had sent to Lhasa took a message from myself and my Cabinet, in which we told Ngabo he should open negotiations on the firm condition that the Chinese armies would not advance any further into Tibet. We had understood that the negotiations would be held either in Lhasa or in Chamdo, where the Chinese armies were stationed, but the Chinese ambassador in India proposed that our delegation should go to Peking. I appointed four more officials as assistants to Ngabo, and they all arrived in Peking at the beginning of 1951.

It was not until they returned to Lhasa, long afterwards, that we heard exactly what had happened to them. According to the report which they submitted then, the Chinese foreign minister Chou En-lai had invited them all to a party when they arrived, and formally introduced them to the Chinese representatives. But as soon as the first meeting began, the chief Chinese representative produced a draft agreement containing ten articles ready-made. This was discussed for several days. Our delegation argued that Tibet was an independent state, and produced all the evidence to support their argument, but the Chinese would not accept it. Ultimately, the Chinese drafted a revised agreement, with seventeen articles. This was presented as an ultimatum. Our delegates were not allowed to make any alterations or suggestions.

They were insulted and abused and threatened with personal violence, and with further military action against the people of Tibet, and they were not allowed to refer to me or my government for further instructions.

This draft agreement was based on the assumption that Tibet was part of China. That was simply untrue, and it could not possibly have been accepted by our delegation without reference to me and my government, except under duress. But Ngabo had been a prisoner of the Chinese for a long time, and the other delegates were also virtual prisoners. At last, isolated from any advice, they yielded to compulsion and signed the document. They still refused to affix the seals which were needed to validate it. But the Chinese forged duplicate Tibetan seals in Peking, and forced our delegation to seal the document with them.

Neither I nor my government were told that an agreement had been signed. We first came to know of it from a broadcast which Ngabo made on Peking Radio. It was a terrible shock when we heard the terms of it. We were appalled at the mixture of Communist clichés, vainglorious assertions which were completely false, and bold statements which were only partly true. And the terms were far worse and more oppressive than anything we had imagined.

The preamble said that "over the last one hundred years or more," imperialist forces had penetrated into China and Tibet and "carried out all kinds of deceptions and provocations," and that "under such conditions, the Tibetan nationality and people were plunged into the depths of enslavement and suffering." This was pure nonsense. It admitted that the Chinese government had ordered the "People's Liberation Army" to march into Tibet. Among the reasons given were that the influence of aggressive imperialist forces in Tibet might be successfully eliminated, and that the Tibetan people might be freed and return to the "big family" of the People's Republic of China.

That was also the subject of Clause One of the agree-

ment: "The Tibetan people shall unite and drive out imperialist aggressive forces from Tibet. The Tibetan people shall
return to the big family of the Motherland—the People's Republic of China." Reading this, we reflected bitterly that
there had been no foreign forces whatever in Tibet since we
drove out the last of the Chinese forces in 1912. Clause Two
provided that "the local government of Tibet shall actively
assist the People's Liberation Army to enter Tibet and con-
solidate the national defense." This in itself went beyond the
specific limits we had placed on Ngabo's authority. Clause
Eight provided for the absorption of the Tibetan army into
the Chinese army. Clause Fourteen deprived Tibet of all authority in external affairs.

In between these clauses which no Tibetan would ever
willingly accept were others in which the Chinese made
many promises: not to alter the existing political system in
Tibet; not to alter the status, functions, and powers of the
Dalai Lama; to respect the religious beliefs, customs, and
habits of the Tibetan people and protect the monasteries; to
develop agriculture and improve the people's standard of living; and not to compel the people to accept reforms. But
these promises were small comfort beside the fact that we
were expected to hand ourselves and our country over to
China and cease to exist as a nation. Yet we were helpless.
Without friends there was nothing we could do but acquiesce, submit to the Chinese dictates in spite of our strong
opposition, and swallow our resentment. We could only hope
that the Chinese would keep their side of this forced, one-
sided bargain.

Soon after the agreement was signed, our delegation sent
a telegram to tell me that the Chinese government had appointed a general called Chang Chin-wu as their representative in Lhasa. He was coming via India, instead of the
long overland route through eastern Tibet. Yatung, where I
was staying, was just inside the Tibetan border on the main

route from India to Lhasa, and so it was clear that I would
have to meet him as soon as he set foot in our country.

I was not looking forward to it. I had never seen a Chinese general, and it was a rather forbidding prospect. Nobody could know how he would behave—whether he would
be sympathetic, or arrive as a conqueror. Some of my officials, ever since the agreement had been signed, had thought
I should go to India for safety before it was too late, and it
had only been after some argument that everyone agreed I
should wait until the general came, and see what his attitude was before we decided.

Some of my senior officials met him in Yatung. I was
staying in a nearby monastery. There was a beautiful pavilion on the roof of the monastery, and we had arranged that
I should meet him there. He insisted in Yatung that he and
I should meet on equal terms, and we got over any difficulties of protocol by providing chairs of equal merit for
everybody, instead of the cushions which were the custom
in Tibet.

When the time came, I was peering out of a window to
see what he looked like. I do not know exactly what I expected, but what I saw was three men in gray suits and
peaked caps who looked extremely drab and insignificant
among the splendid figures of my officials in their red and
golden robes. Had I but known, the drabness was the state
to which China was to reduce us all before the end, and the
insignificance was certainly an illusion.

But when the procession had reached the monastery and
climbed up to my pavilion, the general turned out to be
friendly and informal. The other two gray-coated men were
his aide and his interpreter. He gave me a letter from Mao
Tse-tung, which more or less repeated the first clause of the
agreement by welcoming us back to the great motherland,
a phrase I had already come to detest. Then he said the same
thing all over again through his interpreter. I gave him tea,
and an observer who had not known what was in our hearts

might have thought the whole meeting was perfectly cordial.

His arrival in Lhasa was not so successful. I sent instructions to the Cabinet that he would have to be properly received and treated as a guest of the government. So two members of the Cabinet went out beyond the Norbulingka to meet him with suitable ceremony, and on the following day the Prime Ministers and the Cabinet gave a dinner party in his honor. But that did not satisfy him. He complained that he had not been given the reception due to the representative of a friendly power. So we were made to see that he was not quite as wholeheartedly friendly as he looked.

However, under these circumstances I was compelled to go back to the Norbulingka, and there I witnessed the next extensions of Chinese military rule.

Two months after the arrival of General Chang Chin-wu, three thousand officers and men of the Chinese army marched into Lhasa. Soon after that, another detachment of about the same size arrived there, under two more Generals, Tang Ko-hwa and Tang Kuan-sen. The people of Lhasa watched them come with the apparent indifference which I believe is usually shown at first by ordinary people in the face of such national humiliation. At first there was no contact between the Chinese commanders and our government except when the Chinese demanded supplies and accommodations. But these demands soon began to cause havoc in the city.

The Chinese requisitioned houses, and bought or rented others; and beyond the Ngabo, in the pleasant land beside the river which had always been the favorite place for summer picnics, they took possession of an enormous area for a camp. They demanded a loan of 2,000 tons of barley. This huge amount could not be met from the state granaries at that time because of heavy expenditure, and the government had to borrow from monasteries and private owners. Other kinds of food were also demanded, and the humble resources of the city began to be strained, and prices began to rise.

And then another general, and another eight to ten thousand men appeared. They seized a further area for camps, and under the burden of their extra demands for food our simple economy broke down. They had brought nothing with them, and all expected to be fed from our meager sources of supply. The prices of food-grains suddenly soared up about ten times; of butter, nine times; and of goods in general, two or three times. For the first time that could be remembered, the people of Lhasa were reduced to the edge of famine. Their resentment grew against the Chinese army, and children began to go about shouting slogans and throwing stones at the Chinese soldiers—a sign that the adults were barely keeping their own bitterness in check. Complaints began to pour in to the offices of the Cabinet, but nothing could be done. The Chinese armies had come to stay, and they would not accept any suggestions, or help our government in any way at all. On the contrary, their demands went on increasing every day. Soon they demanded another 2,000 tons of barley, and it had to be found. It was called a loan, and the Generals promised to repay it by investing its value in the development of industries in Tibet, but that promise was never fulfilled.

While conditions were going from bad to worse for the people of Lhasa, high Chinese officials were constantly arriving in the city, and a long series of meetings was convened by General Chang Chin-wu. Members of my Cabinet were requested to attend them, and it fell mostly to Lukhangwa, as my lay Prime Minister, to try to find a balance between the essential needs of the people and the requests of the invaders. He had the courage to tell the Chinese plainly that Tibetans were a humble religious community, whose production had always been just sufficient for their own needs. There was very little surplus—perhaps enough to support the Chinese armies for another month or two, but no more—and a surplus could not be created suddenly. There was no possible reason, he pointed out, for keeping such enormous forces in Lhasa. If they were needed to defend the country, they should be sent to the frontiers, and only officials, with a reasonable escort, should remain in the city.

The Chinese answers were very polite at first. General Chang Chin-wu said that our government had signed the agreement that Chinese forces should be stationed in Tibet, and we were therefore obliged to provide them with accommodation and supplies. He said that they had only come to help Tibet to develop her resources and to protect her against imperialist domination, and that they would go back to China as soon as Tibet was able to administer her own affairs and protect her own frontiers. "When you can stand on your own feet," he said, "we will not stay here even if you ask us to."

Lukhangwa forebore to point out that the only people who had ever threatened our frontiers were the Chinese themselves, and that we had administered our own affairs for centuries. But at another meeting he told the General that in spite of his assurance that the Chinese had come to help Tibet, they had so far done nothing at all to help. On the contrary, their presence was a serious hardship, and most of their actions were bound to add to the anger and resentment of the people. One action he mentioned, more important to us than it may appear, was the burning of the bones of dead animals within the Holy City of Lhasa: this was very offensive to the religious feelings of Tibetans, and had caused a great deal of hostile comment.

But rather than discuss the causes of the people's obvious hostility, Chang Chin-wu expected our government to put an end to it. Among other complaints, he said that people were going about in the streets of Lhasa singing songs in disparagement of the Chinese. He suggested that our government should issue a declaration calling for friendly relations with the Chinese, and he wrote a draft and handed it to Lukhangwa. When Lukhangwa read it, he found it was an order putting a ban on singing in the streets; and of course, rather than issue anything so ludicrous, he rewrote it in a somewhat more dignified form. I do not think the Chinese ever forgave him for that.

Throughout the series of meetings, Chinese complaints grew more forceful. Although they were trying to make it clear to the people, they said, that they had only come to Tibet to help the Tibetans, the behavior of the people was deteriorating every day. They said that public meetings were being held to criticize the Chinese authorities, which no doubt was true, and they requested the Cabinet to put a ban on meetings. That was done, but the people of Lhasa immediately began to put up posters and circulate pamphlets in the city, saying that they were facing starvation and asking the Chinese to go back to China. And in spite of the ban, a large meeting was held at which a memorandum was written setting forth the people's grievances, pointing out that conditions in Lhasa were very serious, and asking that the Chinese troops should be withdrawn and only a few officials be left in the city. One copy of this memorandum was sent to the Chinese generals, and one to the Cabinet. The Chinese said the document was due to the incitement of imperialists, and began to hint that there were certain people in Lhasa who were deliberately creating trouble. On one occasion, Chang Chin-wu came to the Cabinet office and angrily accused the two Prime Ministers of being the leaders of a conspiracy to violate the agreement which had been signed in Peking.

The pattern of these events will be distressingly familiar in any country which has been the victim of invasion. The invaders had arrived believing—with how much sincerity one cannot tell—that they had come as benefactors. They seemed to be surprised to find that the invaded people did not want their benefactions in the least. As popular resentment grew against them, they did not try to allay it by withdrawing, or even by making concessions to the people's wishes. They tried to repress it by ever-increasing force, and rather than blame themselves, they searched for scapegoats. In Tibet, the first scapegoats were purely imaginary "imperialists," and my Prime Minister, Lukhangwa. But this course of action can never lead to anything but disaster. Popular resentment can never be repressed for more than a short time by force, because forceful repression always makes it stronger. This lesson, which one would have thought so obvious, has yet to be learned by the Chinese.

All through this period of mounting tension, the Chinese insisted from time to time on by-passing my Cabinet and the usual agencies of the government and making direct approaches to me. At the beginning, my two Prime Ministers had always been present to advise me when I met the Chinese generals, but at one meeting Chang Chin-wu entirely lost his temper at something my monk Prime Minister Losang Tashi said. It was rather a shock to me at that age. I had never seen a grown man behave like that before. But young though I was, it was I who had to intervene to calm him down; and it was after that that they started demanding to see me alone. Whenever they came to see me, they brought an escort of guards who were stationed outside my room during the interview. This display of bad manners, if it was nothing more, intensely offended the Tibetans who knew of it.

The final crisis between the Chinese and Lukhangwa arose over a matter which had nothing to do with the sufferings of Lhasa. An especially large meeting was called by Chang Chin-wu. My Prime Ministers and Cabinet were summoned, and all the highest Chinese officials, both civil and military, were present. The General announced that the time had come for Tibetan troops to be absorbed in the "People's Liberation Army" under the terms of the Seventeen-Point Agreement, and he proposed that as a first step a number of young Tibetan soldiers should be chosen for training at the Chinese army headquarters in Lhasa. Then, he said, they could go back to their regiments and train the others.

At this, Lukhangwa spoke out more strongly than he ever had before. He said the suggestion was neither necessary nor acceptable. It was absurd to refer to the terms of the Seventeen-Point Agreement. Our people did not accept the agreement and the Chinese themselves had repeatedly broken the terms of it. Their army was still in occupation of eastern Tibet; the area had not been returned to the government of Tibet, as it should have been. The attack on Tibet was totally unjustifiable: the Chinese army had forcibly entered Tibetan territory while peaceful negotiations were actually going on. As for absorbing Tibetan troops in the Chinese army, the agreement had said the Chinese government would not compel Tibetans to accept reforms. This was a reform which the people of Tibet would resent very strongly, and he as Prime Minister would not approve it.

The Chinese generals replied softly that the matter, after all, was not of very great importance, and they could see why the Tibetan government should object to it. Then they slightly changed their ground. They proposed that the Tibetan flag should be hauled down on all Tibetan barracks, and the Chinese flag should be hoisted there instead. Lukhangwa said that if Chinese flags were hoisted on the barracks, the soldiers would certainly pull them down again, which would be embarrassing for the Chinese. In the course of this argument about the flags, Lukhangwa said outright that it was absurd for the Chinese, after violating the integrity of Tibet, to ask Tibetans to have friendly relations with them. "If you hit a man on the head and break his skull," he said, "you can hardly expect him to be friendly." This thoroughly angered the Chinese. They closed the meeting, and proposed to hold another one three days later.

When all the representatives met again, another general, Fan Ming, acted as the Chinese spokesman. He asked Lukhangwa whether he had not been mistaken in his statements at the earlier meeting, no doubt expecting an apology. But Lukhangwa, of course, stood by all that he had said. It was his duty, he added, to explain the situation frankly, because rumors had spread throughout Tibet of Chinese oppressions in the eastern provinces, and feelings were running high. If the Chinese proposals about the army were accepted, the reaction would certainly be violent, not only from the army but from the Tibetan people in general.

At this reply, General Fan Ming lost his temper, and accused Lukhangwa of having clandestine relations with foreign imperialist powers, and shouted that he would request me to dismiss Lukhangwa from his office. Lukhangwa told him that of course if I, the Dalai Lama, were satisfied that he had done any wrong, he would not only give up his office but also his life. Then General Chang Chin-wu intervened to say that Fan Ming was mistaken, and to ask our representatives not to take what he said too seriously. The meeting broke up again without agreement.

Nevertheless, in spite of the soothing intervention of Chang Chin-wu, I received a written report soon after this meeting, in which the Chinese insisted that Lukhangwa did not want to improve relations between Tibet and China, and suggested that he should be removed from office. They made the same demand to the Cabinet, and the Cabinet also expressed the opinion to me that it would be better if both Prime Ministers were asked to resign. So the crisis was brought to a head, and I was faced with a very difficult decision. I greatly admired Lukhangwa's courage in standing up to the Chinese, but now I had to decide whether to let him continue, or whether to bow yet again to a Chinese demand.

There were two considerations: Lukhangwa's personal safety, and the future of our country as a whole. On the first, I had no doubt. Lukhangwa had already put his own life in danger. If I refused to relieve him of office, there was every chance that the Chinese would get rid of him in ways of their own.

On the more general question, my views had evolved

throughout this long period of tension. I had still had no theoretical training in the intricacies of international politics. I could only apply my religious training to these problems, aided I trust by common sense. But religious training, I believed and still believe, was a very reliable guide.

I reasoned that if we continued to oppose and anger the Chinese authorities, it could only lead us further along the vicious circle of repression and popular resentment. In the end, it was certain to lead to outbreaks of physical violence. Yet violence was useless; we could not possibly get rid of the Chinese by any violent means. They would always win if we fought them, and our own unarmed and unorganized people would be the victims. Our only hope was to persuade the Chinese peaceably to fulfill the promises they had made in their agreement. Nonviolence was the only course which might win us back a degree of freedom in the end, perhaps after years of patience. That meant cooperation whenever it was possible, and passive resistance whenever it was not.

And violent opposition was not only unpractical, it was also unethical. Nonviolence was the only moral course. This was not only my own profound belief, it was also clearly in accordance with the teaching of Lord Buddha, and as the religious leader of Tibet I was bound to uphold it. We might be humiliated, and our most cherished inheritances might seem to be lost for a period, but if so, humility must be our portion. I was certain of that.

So I sadly accepted the Cabinet's recommendation and asked the Prime Ministers to resign. They came to call on me, and I gave them scarves and gifts and my photograph. I felt that they understood my position very well. I did not appoint any successors. It was no use having Prime Ministers if they were merely scapegoats for the Chinese. It was better that I should accept the responsibilities myself, because my position was unassailable in the eyes of all Tibetans. Later, Lukhangwa went to India and became my Prime Minister in exile until his advancing age made him retire, and he is still my trusted advisor. But it grieves me to say that in 1959, after I left Tibet myself, Losang Tashi, the monk Prime Minister, was thrown into prison by the Chinese and has not been released.

When that incident came to an end, the attitude of the Chinese became more friendly and conciliatory. They suggested to the Cabinet that a delegation of Tibetan officials, monks, merchants, and other people should be sent to China to see for themselves, as they put it, that the people of China had absolute freedom to practice their religion. We accepted this suggestion, and chose members for a delegation. They were taken on a conducted tour of China, and when they came back they submitted a report which everybody knew had been written under Chinese orders.

And then I myself was invited by the Chinese government to visit China. Although there had certainly been a slight improvement in relations between my government and the Chinese authorities in Tibet, I was still greatly disappointed at their complete disregard for the interests and welfare of our people. I thought I ought to meet the highest authorities in China, and try to persuade them to carry out the promises they had made in the agreement they had forced on us. So I decided to go.

6

IN COMMUNIST CHINA

The people of Lhasa were very unwilling that I should go to China. They were afraid I might never be allowed to come back. But I had no fear of being kept prisoner, and I had made up my mind that it was my duty to go. Therefore, at a religious ceremony in the Norbulingka, when there were a great many people present, I did my best to reassure them by promising to be home within a year.

At that time, a session of the Chinese People's National Assembly was being prepared in Peking to frame a constitution, and the Chinese had allotted ten seats in the assembly to Tibet. The Chinese representatives were said to have been elected, but I had been asked to nominate the Tibetan members, and the Chinese government had suggested that I should lead the delegation myself. Many of our people thought it was not in keeping with the dignity of the Dalai Lama to be a member of such an assembly, but it seemed to me there was nothing to be gained by refusing. On the contrary, if we refused we might lose whatever chance of autonomy we possessed; whereas, to agree might possibly help in persuading the Chinese to keep their promises.

So I left Lhasa in 1954. A religious ceremony was held on the bank of the river, where the people of Lhasa gathered to bid me good-by. Evidently they were very sad and depressed at my going, and I myself could not look forward with any pleasure to my first journey out of Tibet.

I was able to start the long journey by car. The Chinese had managed to bring many vehicles, mostly military, into Lhasa, and strategic roads were being built from the east and northwest. The road-building had been another source of oppression and discontent. Tibetan workers had been conscripted, because none would volunteer, and their pay was extremely small. Land had been requisitioned, largely without compensation. Where arable lands were taken, our government had been told to provide other land for the dispossessed peasant farmers, but usually, no other fertile land could be found in the same neighborhood. If our country had to be developed, no doubt roads were a necessity, but the way the Chinese built them was an injustice and affront to the country people.

We drove for the first ninety miles out of Lhasa. Beyond that, the road was only half completed, and we had to go on horseback again, as Tibetans had always been content to travel. There had been heavy rainfall, and there were several landslides across the foundations of the road. In some places, we could not ride, but had to wade through mud. And where the road ran along the mountainsides, boulders were hurtling down from above, across the road, and falling into the river hundreds of feet below. The half-built road was so dangerous that three people were killed on our journey—also many mules and horses.

Then, for another ten days, we were able to travel by jeep, although the road was still very rough. For the last six of these days, we were passing through an area which was predominantly Tibetan, although, like my own home district, it had been seized by the Chinese long ago and kept under Chinese rule. The people were mostly descendants of the original Tibetan stock, and wherever I stopped for the night I had to give public audiences. They were all insistent that on my way back from China I should stay a few days among them.

At the place called Tachienlu we crossed the hill, famous in Tibetan history, which marked the ancient original border between Tibet and China. On the other side, we could see at once that we were really in a foreign country. The people were Chinese in appearance—their houses, their dress, their attitude and manners were all entirely different. And we began to pass tea houses by the roadside—a certain sign that we were now in China itself. We drove on all the way to the Chinese town of Chengtu. Then we flew to Sian, and from there went by special train to Peking.

Only a few years before, when mechanical things so interested me, flying or traveling by train would have seemed like a glorious dream. But now that I was doing them both for the first time, my mind was much too full of our political misfortunes and my responsibility for me to enjoy these new experiences.

At Sian, the Panchen Lama joined us. He was younger than I was, though people often said he looked older. I was nineteen then, and he was sixteen. He had grown up in an almost impossibly difficult situation.

The Panchen Lamas, like the Dalai Lamas, are high incarnates. The first incarnation of both took place in the fourteenth Christian century. Ever since, the Panchen Lamas had been among the lamas second only to the Dalai Lamas in religious authority in Tibet, but they had never held any secular authority. Throughout our history, relations between the two had been perfectly cordial, as befitted high religious leaders. In most generations, the younger had become the pupil of the older.

But a rift began between our two immediate predecessors

in about 1910, at the time when the Chinese invaded Tibet and the Thirteenth Dalai Lama had to flee to India. Some of the attendants of the Panchen Lama of that time took the opportunity of the Dalai Lama's absence to complain about the taxes levied by the government, and about other similar secular matters. The Chinese, seeing the incipient disagreement, did all that they could to widen it, in the hope, no doubt, of dividing Tibet and making it an easier prey to their attack. They failed to divide Tibet, as I have already told, and the Tibetans drove them out of the country. But the rift between the two Lamas persisted, and a few years later the Panchen Lama went to the Chinese-controlled territory on the frontier. There he lived for the rest of his life, and died, I believe in sorrow, in 1937.

In these circumstances, it was an unusually long time before the search was made for his reincarnation. In 1950, two possible candidates had been discovered in Tibet itself, and the Chinese themselves had put forward a candidate in the territory they ruled. During the negotiations in Peking which ended in the so-called agreement of 1951, I had a telegram from Ngabo, the leader of our delegation, saying that if the Chinese candidate was not accepted it would hinder his negotiations. Naturally, the government and the monastic leaders wanted to carry out the traditional tests, but that was impossible at the time, and gradually the present Panchen Lama came to be accepted as the true reincarnation. He was then already eleven or twelve.

Of course, the whole of his education and training was subject to Chinese influence, first under the regime of Chiang Kai-shek and then under the Communists. And the Chinese had certainly made use of him for their own political ends, knowing that he was too young to protest. For example, when the Communist government conquered China, a telegram of congratulations to them was sent and published in his name, although he was only ten at the time and had not yet been accepted as the reincarnation; and no doubt many people were deceived into thinking that this telegram came from official Tibetan circles.

I had already met him once before. He came to Lhasa to see me in 1953, when he was fourteen. Of course, he was brought by a retinue of Chinese officials, beside his own monastic followers. He was formally presented to me in the traditional ceremonial way, as my junior not only in age but in position; but I could see at that very first meeting that the Chinese and some of his own officials were not happy with our ancient customs. They would have liked to see the Panchen Lama seated on a level with myself. So that first meeting was constrained and not very successful. But on the same day we met again informally and had lunch together alone, and I must say that we got on well together. He showed a genuine respect for my position, as the custom of Buddhism requires towards a senior monk. He was correct and pleasant in his manners—a true Tibetan, and I had a firm impression of unforced goodwill. I felt sure that left to himself he would have whole-heartedly supported Tibet against the inroads of China.

At the end of his visit to Lhasa, his Chinese escort prevented the customary formal leave-taking, but he came to say good-by to me privately at the Norbulingka. I noticed a difference in his attitude, as if he had been warned in the meantime to behave in a superior manner. But I reminded him how important it was for him, as it was for me, to pursue religious studies, and I suggested that as we were both young we should forget the differences of our predecessors and make a fresh start, and he agreed.

I did sincerely regret those old differences, and I still do. I do not think he was allowed to forget them entirely, because of his continuous Chinese teaching. If he and his followers had done so, Tibet's disaster might have been less complete. The Chinese were trying to do in our generation exactly what they had failed to do in the last; and this time, it has certainly been an advantage to them to have a Tibetan

religious leader in whose name they can make their proclamations. But the Panchen Lama cannot be personally blamed.
No boy who grew up under such concentrated, constant alien
influence could possibly retain his own free will. And in
spite of this influence, I do not believe he will ever quite
abandon our religion in favor of communism.

After we met at Shingnan we traveled on to Peking in
company, and there we were received by the Vice-Chairman,
Chu Te, the Prime Minister, Chou En-lai, and other officials
of the Peking government. There were crowds to welcome
us at the railway station. Most of them looked like students
or members of youth leagues, and they clapped and cheered
us loudly. But I had a cynical feeling that they would have
showed hostility just as readily if that had been what they
had been told to do. It reminded me of a conversation which
was said to have been heard when a Chinese official was
visiting a Tibetan village. The villagers had all assembled
to greet him when he arrived, and they clapped enthusiasti-
cally. Gratified, he asked one of them whether they were
happy under the new regime.

"Yes, quite happy," the Tibetan said.

"That's excellent."

"Except that we don't like this new tax."

"New tax?"

"Yes. The clapping tax. Every time a Chinese comes here,
we all have to turn out and clap."

And remembering that many Tibetan taxes had always
been paid in more or less unpleasant labor, the story has a
ring of truth about it.

On the evening we arrived, Chu Te gave a banquet in
honor of myself and the Panchen Lama. Covers were laid
for 200 people, and everything was on a grand and lavish
scale which really surprised me. The table appointments were
all of the finest quality, and Chinese wines were served,
though of course none of our delegation except a few lay
officials tried them. Chu Te made a speech of welcome, say-

ing that the Tibetans had come back to their motherland, and that the government of China would do its best to help them. It was all quite a new experience for me, and I was not quite sure how I should deal with all the members of the Chinese government. But there was one consolation— everyone was courteous and polite, and seemed to be most cultured and well educated.

Two days later I met Mao Tse-tung for the first time. It was a memorable interview. The meeting was arranged at the House of Reception, where distinguished visitors were usually introduced to the Chairman of the Chinese Communist Party. Mao Tse-tung had several people in attendance, including Liu Shao-chi, who is now President of the Republic, and I had four or five officials with me.

Mao Tse-tung began by saying that he was glad Tibet had come back to the Motherland and that I had agreed to take part in the National Assembly. He said it was the mission of China to bring progress to Tibet by developing its natural resources, and that the generals who were in Lhasa, Chang Chin-wu and Fan Ming, were there as representatives of China to help me and the people of Tibet. They had not gone there to exercise any kind of authority over the Tibetan government or people. And he asked me point blank whether these Chinese representatives had done anything against my wishes.

I felt I was in a very difficult position. I was sure that unless I could maintain a friendly atmosphere, our country would suffer far more than it had already. So I told him that the people of Tibet had great hopes for their future under his leadership, and therefore, whenever there had been differences with the Chinese representatives, we had expressed our opinions frankly.

My next interview with him lasted for about three hours, and there was nobody present except an interpreter. Again, of course, we talked mostly about Tibet and its future. I gave him a personal account of the recent events in Tibet, trying to dispel any doubts he might have had about our situation. I wanted to create a feeling of confidence in his mind, because I was still convinced that we could not get rid of the Chinese rule simply by uncompromising opposition to it. We could only hope to alleviate it and try patiently to make it evolve into something tolerable.

I had been told by the members of a Tibetan trade delegation which visited China in 1953 that the Chinese Communist leaders had serious doubts about me, mainly because of the treasure I had deposited in India, and because they seemed to think that some members of my family had close connections with other foreign powers. That was quite untrue, as it happened, and I took this opportunity to tell Mao Tse-tung so. As for the treasure, the Chinese had often asked me about it, and I always told them I was thinking of bringing it back to Lhasa. And so I was, but luckily I never did.

Mao seemed very pleased with what I told him, and said that at one stage the Chinese government had decided to set up a committee of political and military members to govern Tibet directly under the Chinese government, but now he did not think that would be necessary. Perhaps, I thought, that was one victory for my policy. Instead of that, he added, they had now decided to set up a Preparatory Committee of the Autonomous Region of Tibet. He asked for my opinion, but it was much too big a subject for a quick judgment, and I told him I would not like to make any comments without consulting other Tibetans, including the Panchen Lama.

That led him to mention the misunderstandings between the Panchen Lama and what he insisted on calling the "local government of Tibet." He suggested that as we were both in Peking we should take the opportunity to settle our differences. I told him these differences were a legacy of the past, and that personally I had no difference with the Panchen Lama. If there were any lingering misunderstandings, I would be happy to clear them up.

A few days later I had a message from Mao Tse-tung to

say that he was coming to see me in an hour's time. When he arrived he said he had merely come to call. Then something made him say that Buddhism was quite a good religion, and Lord Buddha, although he was a prince, had given a good deal of thought to the question of improving the conditions of the people. He also observed that the Goddess Tara was a kindhearted woman. After a very few minutes, he left. I was quite bewildered by these remarks and did not know what to make of them.

Once while I was in Peking I had a chance to see him in action as the great leader of Communist China. I was invited to a meeting at his house which was attended by about twenty high officials, and I sat next to him and could feel the impact of his personality. The subject of the meeting was the standard of living of the Chinese peasants. He spoke bluntly and, I thought, with great sincerity, saying that he was not yet satisfied with what was being done in this respect. He quoted letters from his own village saying that Communist officials were not doing all they should to help the people. After a while, he turned to me and said that Tibetans were firm, or stubborn, in their ideas, but that after twenty years Tibet would be strong. Now, China was helping Tibet, but after twenty years Tibet would be helping China. He mentioned the great Chinese military leader Shi Ring-gnow, who had led his armies to many victories but had finally met his match in the Tibetans. Again, I was very surprised by what he said; but this time, at least his remarks were more acceptable.

My final interview with this remarkable man was toward the end of my visit to China. I was at a meeting of the Standing Committee of the National Assembly when I received a message asking me to go to see him at his house. By then, I had been able to complete a tour of the Chinese provinces, and I was able to tell him truthfully that I had been greatly impressed and interested by all the development projects I had seen. Then he started to give me a long lecture about the true form of democracy, and advised me how to become a leader of the people and how to take heed of their suggestions. And then he edged closer to me on his chair and whispered: "I understand you very well. But of course, religion is poison. It has two great defects: It undermines the race, and secondly it retards the progress of the country. Tibet and Mongolia have both been poisoned by it."

I was thoroughly startled; what did he mean to imply? I tried to compose myself, but I did not know how to take him. Of course, I knew he must be a bitter enemy of religion. Yet he seemed to be genuinely friendly and affectionate toward me. He came out to the car with me after these extraordinary remarks, and his parting advice was merely that I should take care of my health.

Before I left China I was greatly impressed by Mao Tsetung's outstanding personality. I met him many times on social occasions, apart from our private meetings. His appearance gave no sign of his intellectual power. He did not look healthy, and was always panting and breathing heavily. His dress was of just the same style as everybody else's, although it was usually a different color; but he did not pay much attention to his clothes, and once I noticed that the cuffs of his shirt were torn. His shoes looked as though they had never been polished. He was slow in his movements, and slower still in speech. He was sparing of words, and spoke in short sentences, each full of meaning and usually clear and precise; and he smoked incessantly while he talked. Yet his manner of speech certainly captured the minds and imaginations of his listeners, and gave the impression of kindness and sincerity. I was sure that he believed what he said, and that he was confident of achieving whatever object he had in view. I was also convinced that he himself would never use force to convert Tibet into a Communist state. Certainly, I was disillusioned afterwards by the policy of persecution which was adopted by the Chinese authorities in Tibet, but I still find it hard to believe that these oppressions had the approval and support of Mao Tse-tung.

Another important man in the Chinese hierarchy was Chou En-lai, the Prime Minister, and I had quite a different impression of him. I had met him for the first time when he came to the railway station to receive me, and I had several brief talks with him during my stay in China. In one of them, he gave me a great deal of advice about the future of Tibet, saying how important it was to build up and develop the country as quickly as possible. I told him we knew that our country had been backward, and that it would now be possible to improve the material conditions of life and modernize the administration. As I have said, I had already started to do this myself. But I added that if our natural resources were to be developed, we would certainly need economic aid at first.

I always found Chou En-lai friendly, but he was not as frank and open as Mao Tse-tung had seemed to be. He was extremely polite, courteous, and suave, and seemed to have complete control of himself, so that I was very surprised to hear a story quite recently of how he had stormed and thumped the table at a meeting in Nepal. The very first time I met him I realized he was very clever and shrewd. I also had the impression that he would be ruthless in carrying out whatever projects he had in hand. I was not in the least surprised, as I would have been with Mao Tse-tung, to learn later that he approved the policy of oppression in Tibet.

While I was in Peking I also met a few distinguished foreigners, but only briefly. I was introduced to the Russian Ambassador at a dinner party and had a short talk with him. He said he would like a much longer interview, and I gladly agreed. But that interview never took place, and I began to understand that the Chinese did not want me to have a chance of speaking frankly to foreigners. Exactly the same thing happened with a Rumanian minister. I did have an interview with the Indian Ambassador. The Chinese could not object to my meeting him, since India was such a close neighbor of ours, but they insisted on sending Chinese interpreters instead of my own to the meeting. My own interpreter could translate very well from Tibetan to English, but the Chinese had to put all I said into Chinese first, so that his colleague could put it into English for the Ambassador. So the atmosphere was formal and constrained, and not very much could be said. There were also two other extremely grave and pompous Chinese officials present. During the meeting, a large bowl of fruit was upset, and my main memory of the occasion is seeing those two very dignified gentlemen on their hands and knees under the table looking for oranges and bananas.

I also had the privilege of meeting Mr. Khrushchev and Mr. Bulganin when they came to Peking to attend the celebrations of the Chinese National Day. I went to the airport to meet them and was introduced to them there, and also met them at a reception the same evening; but we had no discussion or exchange of views.

It was also in Peking that I first had the pleasure of meeting Mr. Nehru, though it was perhaps an inauspicious place for us to meet. It was then that I first learned the danger of being misunderstood by reporters. It has been said that I associated Mr. Nehru with a pro-Chinese policy. That is not correct. I had heard and read a great deal about him, and I was very eager to have a talk with him and seek his advice; but while we were in China I did not succeed. I was introduced to him by Chou En-lai at a cocktail party. He seemed to be absorbed in thought, and for a little while he did not say anything. I told him his name and reputation as a leading statesman of the world had reached us in our isolation in Tibet, and that I had been looking forward to meeting him. He smiled, but only said he was glad to have met me; and though I saw him on other occasions, those were the only words I had with him in China. There were reports that I had private talks with him, but I did not. Nor did he ask me whether there was anything India could do to help Tibet. I was very disappointed not to be able to talk to him, because I very much wanted his help and advice, but that wish was not fulfilled until I went to India the following year.

It was at a reception during Mr. Nehru's visit that a representative of the Indian press came to interview me with a Chinese interpreter. He asked me what I thought of Mr. Nehru's visit to China. I said I hoped the two great countries would come closer together, and so set an example to Asia and the world. Then he asked me whether I was prepared to introduce reforms in Tibet; and I told him that ever since I had come to power in Tibet I had been trying my best to introduce reforms in our political and social life, and that I hoped my efforts would be successful and that he would hear the results of them before very long. But at that stage a Chinese official interrupted us and took me away. I was amused to see the Chinese interpreter hastily taking notes of this conversation, and he told me afterwards that he had orders to write down everything I said and report it to the authorities.

I also gave a dinner party in Peking, to celebrate the Tibetan New Year by returning some of the hospitality I had received. Everything was done according to the traditions and customs of Tibet. On the invitation cards we sent out there were pictures of what are called "The Four United Brothers"—an elephant, a monkey, a rabbit and a bird. The bird, a symbol of auspiciousness, represents Lord Buddha, and the pictures were meant to emphasize, from our own point of view, the "union of the nationalities" which the Chinese were always proclaiming. I had the pleasure of meeting many Chinese officials on this occasion, including Mao Tse-tung, and I was struck again by their charm of manner and courtesy and culture. We had no religious ceremonies at the party, but we had the usual New Year decorations and a special kind of cake which is made in Tibet for this season. It is our custom to take a small piece of this cake and throw it up to the ceiling as an offering to Buddha. When Mao Tse-tung was told of this custom, he threw up a piece to the ceiling, and then with a mischievous expression, he threw another piece down on the floor.

Between these social occasions, there were long meetings of the National Assembly. These were my first experience of political meetings, and what struck me was that so many members showed so little interest in what was going on. I admit I could not take much interest myself. I was tired after the long journey to China, and the proceedings were in Chinese which I could not follow. I would have expected the Chinese themselves to be more alert, but I was sitting near some elderly representatives, and they seemed to be even more tired and bored than I was. The expressions on their faces showed that they could not follow what the discussions were about. They were always watching the clock for the tea break, and when the break was shorter than usual they complained.

I attended many other conferences in China, and my impression was always the same. When speeches were made from the floor they were often irrelevant, and usually mere echoes of the glorification of Communist achievements. When members did express views of their own, it made no difference. A senior member of the party would get up and state the official view, and the Chairman would accept it without allowing more discussion. There were genuine discussions in committees, but not even these affected the party's decisions. In short, the long meetings and conferences were empty formalities, because no mere delegate had the power to bring about changes even if he were interested enough to want to do so.

I found a very different atmosphere when I visited the Indian Parliament the next year. After my Chinese experience of political discussion, it was a very pleasant surprise to hear the ordinary Indian members of parliament speaking frankly and freely, and criticizing the government in the strongest terms. I was so impressed that I spoke to Chou En-lai about it, since he happened to be in New Delhi at the time, but his only answer was that things had entirely changed since my visit to Peking.

I have one other abiding impression of Chinese political meetings: the formidable length of the leaders' speeches. All the leaders seemed to be passionately devoted to oratory, and they never missed a chance to express their views. I especially remember the speech which Chou En-lai gave after he returned from the Bandung Conference. It was while I was on my way back to Tibet and was held up at Chengtu because there had been an earthquake on the road ahead. Chou En-lai and Marshal Chen Yi, a vice-chairman of the Party, also stopped there on their way from the Conference back to China. I was told they were coming, and went to the airfield to meet them. Chou En-lai came to the house where I was staying, and we had a few minutes' talk, and then we went on to the local army hall. There were three or four hundred people there, and he started a speech about the success of the Chinese delegation at the Conference. He spoke of the importance of studying foreign affairs, and told the audience that when he was at the Conference he had met representatives of states he had never heard of, so that he had to look them up in an atlas. That speech went on for five solid hours before we came to the usual ending in the glorification of the achievements of the Communist regime. But Chen Yi probably held the record for speeches. When he started, he usually did not stop for seven hours. Listening to this verbosity, I often wondered what was going on in the minds of the audiences. But these were mostly younger Communists, not the few remaining representatives of the older way of life whom I had seen at the National Assembly; and looking around, I hardly ever saw any sign of boredom or weariness. The patience of most of these people seemed to me to show that their minds had already been reformed and reshaped in the pattern of communism.

I had the same strong impression of a uniform mass mind when I went on tours to different parts of China. I traveled for three months through the country and visited monasteries, industrial plants, workers' organizations, cooperative farms, schools, and universities. I must say that the whole country had an air of efficiency. I met many officials, and I still have very happy recollections of some of them. The best were capable and courteous, and well trained in diplomacy. Government departments were well organized and worked promptly. I must also say that the ignorant workers seemed to be satisfied, and the general conditions of their life seemed, at that time, to be adequate. It was only among the literate people that one ever had a sense of hidden dissatisfaction. Nor could anyone deny the enormous industrial progress which China had made under communism.

But even the merits of efficiency and progress must be balanced against their cost, and it seemed to me that in China the cost was formidable. Progress had cost the people all their individuality. They were becoming a mere homogeneous mass of humanity. Everywhere I went I found them strictly organized, disciplined, and controlled, so that they not only all dressed the same—men and women dressed in drab dungarees—but all spoke and behaved the same, and I believe all thought the same. They could hardly do otherwise, because they only had one source of information—the newspapers and radio published only the government's version of the news. Foreign papers and radio were prohibited. Once when I was going through a village near Peking with a Chinese officer, I was pleasantly surprised to hear European music, which sounded like the music broadcast by the BBC before its news bulletins. And the startled expression on my escort's face was most revealing. The people even seemed to have lost the habit of laughing spontaneously; they only seemed to laugh when they were supposed to laugh, and to sing when they were told to sing. Certainly some of the young Communists were clever and well educated, in their fashion, but they never expressed original opinions. It was always the same story of the greatness of China and her glorious achievements. Even in Sining, near the place where I was born on the borders of Tibet, one of the leaders of the local Party gave me a long lecture which was exactly the same thing I had heard so often in Peking. But he did make one original remark: "Except for Russia," he said, "China is the greatest country in the world. It is the only country so great that you have to travel all day and night in a train to cross it."

This was the general impression left upon me by nearly a year in China: efficiency and material progress, and a gray fog of humorless uniformity, through which the traditional charm and courtesy of old China occasionally shone in surprising and welcome gleam. Such utter uniformity, of course, is the formidable strength of communism. But I could not believe that the Chinese would ever succeed in reducing Tibetans to such a slavish state of mind. Religion, humor, and individuality are the breath of life to Tibetans, and no Tibetan would ever willingly exchange these qualities for mere material progress, even if the exchange did not also involve subjection to an alien race.

As I prepared for my journey back to Lhasa, I still had hopes of saving my people from the worst consequences of Chinese domination. I thought my visit to China had helped in two ways. It had certainly shown me exactly what we were up against, and, which was more important, it seemed to have persuaded the Chinese not to go ahead with the original plan, which Mao Tse-tung had admitted, of governing us directly from Peking through a military and political committee. Instead, we seemed to have been left with some authority over our own internal affairs, and we seemed to have a firm promise of autonomy.

By then, I had learned the details of the "Preparatory Committee for the Tibet Autonomous Region" which Mao Tse-tung had proposed as an alternative. It was to have fifty-one members, of whom all except five would be Tibetans. I was to be chairman, and the Panchen Lama and a Chinese official were to be vice-chairmen. Ngabo was secretary-general. The Committee's task was to prepare for regional autonomy in Tibet, by setting up sub-committees for economic and religious affairs, corresponding apparently to our *Tse-khang* and *Yig-tsang,* and the usual departments of government.

It was true that members of the Committee were to be chosen in an anomalous way. Only fifteen members, including myself, were to represent the "Tibetan local government"—that is, our own true government. Eleven were to be chosen from among the leading monasteries, religious sects, public bodies, and prominent people. And ten each were to represent two separate bodies created by the Chinese: the "Chamdo Liberation Committee," which they had set up in the eastern district which had first been invaded and never returned to our government; and the "Panchen Lama's Committee," which they had created in a western area of Tibet where they were trying to give the Panchen Lama the secular authority his predecessors had never possessed. The remaining five members were to be Chinese officials in Lhasa, and all the appointments were to be subject to the approval of the Chinese government.

To give membership to these separate newly invented regions was an infringement in itself of the Chinese agreement not to alter the political system in Tibet or the status of the Dalai Lama. And the choice of members already had the seeds in it of failure. But people in desperate situations are always ready to cling to the slightest hope, and I hoped—in spite of my gloomy experience of Chinese political committees—that a committee with forty-six Tibetan members and only five Chinese could be made to work.

So I set off for home, very anxious to see what had been happening there, and trusting that we could make good use of this last degree of freedom.

▣ 7 ▣

REPRESSION AND RESENTMENT

It was on my way home that I had the chance to visit Taktser again, the village where I was born. That was a moment of happiness in a journey of foreboding. I was proud and thankful to remember that I had been born in a humble and truly Tibetan family, and I enjoyed reviving my faint memories of the places I had left when I was four. But whenever I spoke to the people, I was brought back abruptly to the present. I asked them if they were happy, and they answered that they were "very happy and prosperous under the guidance of the Chinese Communist Party and Chairman Mao Tse-tung." But even while they said it, I saw tears in their eyes, and I realized with a shock that even to me they were afraid to answer the question except by this Chinese Communist formula.

But in one of the neighboring monasteries, I had some long talks with the lamas, and of course they had the confidence to be more outspoken. I found them very anxious. The Chinese had already started to enforce collective farming, and the peasants bitterly resented it. The lamas foresaw that the Chinese would take more and more drastic action to compel the peasants to accept their schemes. I spoke also to several of the lay leaders of the people, and they told me of other Communist "reforms," and said that tension was growing and that the Chinese were becoming more oppressive and suspicious. I made a point of meeting the Chinese officials too, and told them that although reforms were necessary, they should not be the same as the reforms in China, and should not be enforced but only introduced by degrees, with consideration for the local circumstances and the wishes and habits of the people. But I was distressed to find that the Chinese here, so far from Peking, were rude and completely unsympathetic. They simply meant to ignore the people's feelings. One Chinese general even went so far as to tell me they were bringing extra troops into the district in order to enforce their reforms, no matter what the people wanted. Evidently the future for our Tibetan people in this Chinese territory was very black indeed.

Yet these people remained entirely Tibetan in character. As I passed through, stopping here and there for two or three days, sometimes in Chinese official rest houses and sometimes in monasteries, no less than 100,000 people came in from all over the district to see me and pay their respect.

While I was in Peking, a delegation had come to ask me to visit a great many places in eastern Tibet on my journey home. As I was delayed by the earthquake which damaged the road ahead, I did not have time to go everywhere I would have liked. I went to all the monasteries I could reach by car, and to the others I sent three of the highest lamas in my company to represent me: Trijang Rinpoché (my Junior Tutor), Chung Rinpoché, and Karma-pa, the present reincarnation of the same Karma-pa whose fourth reincarnation founded the monastery on the mountain above my village.

All the way through these border areas, I found the same heavy air of foreboding. Among the Tibetans, I saw mounting bitterness and hatred of Chinese; and among the Chinese, I saw the mounting ruthlessness and resolution which is born of fear and lack of understanding. To the Chinese I urged moderation with all the emphasis I could; and to Tibetans I often spoke at meetings, telling them that they should remain united, try to improve things by all peaceful means, and accept whatever was good in Chinese methods. This advice was the only hope, I felt, of averting violence. But now that I had seen how mutual enmity had grown in the year since I passed that way, I had to admit to myself that the hope was slender.

At last I passed the river called Di-chu (the Ghost River), which marked the boundary between Tibet and China, and entered the Chamdo region where the invasion had begun. I spent a few days at the Chinese headquarters in the town of Chamdo, and a few days more at the monastery. This was the district where the Chinese had set up the Chamdo Liberation Committee, with which I was expected to cooperate in future. It had some Tibetan members, but I soon saw that it was the Chinese officials who had all the authority, and that the district was ruled in practice by the general commanding the army. Here also resentment was boiling, and people told me stories of oppressions and injustices, of peasants dispossessed of land, and of promises which the Tibetans had believed at first but the Chinese had always broken. And here was an added danger of sudden violence: This was the district where the Khampas lived, and the most precious possession of a Khampa, as I have said, was his rifle. Now the Khampas had heard that the Chinese were going to demand that all arms should be surrendered, and I knew, without being told, that a Khampa would never surrender his rifle—he would use it first.

Here also, people came in by tens of thousands to pay their respect to me, and when I welcomed them I told them

I was happy to see their spirit of patriotism. I said there had been defects in the way Tibetan officials of the central Tibetan government had behaved there in the past, and that was at least one reason why they had had to suffer the ordeal of invasion. Now, I said, the duty of all Tibetans was to remain united, and then, when the Preparatory Committee began to function, Chamdo would again be an integral part of our country.

My journey through the border areas reminded me of two of my observations in China itself, one very sad and the other revealing a remaining ray of hope.

The first was of Chinese monasteries. In all the remoter parts of China, I had found the temples and monasteries neglected and almost empty, even those of great historical importance. The few remaining monks in them were old, and were living under such suspicion that very few people dared to come to the temples to pray or make offerings. I did not find much learning left among the monks, although I was told there were still learned lamas in Inner Mongolia; and indeed, while I was in Peking, several hundred people came from Inner Mongolia to ask for my blessing. But young people were discouraged from joining monastic orders, and religious organizations had been so effectively penetrated by Communists that even they were being used to spread political propaganda. The Chinese government said their people had religious freedom, but one could see that no future was planned for religious foundations. They were being starved to death and allowed to decay.

This was the fate I could see hanging over the Tibetan monks and monasteries already in Chinese hands. But my other observation gave me some hope that it still might be averted. I had seen splendid evidence that Tibetans, young and old, were too stable in their character and beliefs to be an easy prey for Chinese indoctrination. Tibetan boys had been taken to what was called the School of Nationalities in Peking, together with boys from Mongolia, East Turkestan, and Korea; and the Chinese made every effort there to purge their minds of their own religious and cultural traditions, and to fill them with the new ideas of the dictatorship of the State. But I was glad to find that the minds of the Tibetan boys had not been imprisoned. They still cherished our own ideals, and their national spirit could not be destroyed. In the end, the Chinese gave up trying to convert them, and later these boys found their way back home. Some of them lost their lives in the revolt against the Chinese rule in Lhasa; and a few, still under the age of twenty, became refugees in India. After that failure, the Chinese opened several other schools in the border country, but there too they had no success at all. Tibetan children simply would not swallow their materialistic creed, but remained Tibetans and Buddhists in all their inmost thoughts. I believe boys from Mongolia and East Turkestan clung equally stubbornly to their faith. No doubt this was the reason why, in later years, the Chinese started to seize Tibetan babies a few weeks old and take them away to China, in the hope that they would grow up into Tibetan Communists. But in the meantime, I was greatly encouraged by the depth of the faith of these young Tibetans, and I felt that whatever the Chinese did to us they would never destroy us completely.

It was still quite an adventurous journey from China to Tibet on the new Chinese military road. It had been raining heavily, the rivers were in flood, and there were many landslides and falls of rock. I have a very vivid mental image of one dark night in pouring rain when our convoy was halted by a damaged bridge exactly at a spot where boulders were crashing down on the road from the mountainside above. The Chinese rushed about in confusion, shouting, we Tibetans sat in our canvas-covered jeeps and said our prayers. And earlier that same day, we had had a rather narrow escape from a worse disaster. We had come to a bridge which had collapsed at one end. The Chinese had patched it up and thought we could cross it, but they advised us to lighten the load by walking across and waiting for the convoy. So we did, and we stood and watched our jeeps and trucks begin to cross. A few came over safely, and then, just as the wheels of a jeep came onto the bridge, there were loud cracks and sounds of splintering timber and the bridge broke up and fell into the torrent underneath. Luckily, the driver heard the noise, and reversed very quickly and saved himself. But more than half of our convoy, with all our dry clothes and bedding, was left on the wrong side of the river. We packed ourselves into the vehicles which had crossed, and spent a cold and uncomfortable night at a Chinese rest house.

At last I came home to Lhasa. I cannot say how thankful I was to be in the Norbulingka again. Close outside its walls, the Chinese military camp still menaced us, but inside, all was still calm and beautiful, and our religious practices continued almost undisturbed.

I found that my Cabinet was still maintaining tolerably friendly relations with the Chinese, and the hostility of the Lhasan people seemed to have died down and given way to a feeling of complacency. The city was quiet and peaceful. The people did not know of the drastic changes which were being enforced in the eastern border areas. The bitter resentment I had seen there had not yet spread with its full force into central Tibet. So it seemed that there might still be time for the Preparatory Committee to do some useful work and prevent the worst.

The Chinese government was sending Marshal Chen Yi, the deputy Prime Minister distinguished for seven-hour speeches, to preside at the inauguration of the Committee. The Chinese wanted me to go to receive him when he arrived in Lhasa. My Cabinet refused to approve of that, but I felt it was not a time to stand on dignity. If it would please the Marshal and help to give the Committee a better start, I thought it was worth it. So I went.

*   *   *

The inauguration was in April 1956. I attended it with the feeling that here, among these fifty-one members, was the last hope for the peaceful evolution of our country. It did not seem an impossible hope. The constitutional scheme looked sound and attractive. On paper, it had none of the absolutely unacceptable aspects of communism. And, with such a high proportion of Tibetan members in the Committee, it looked as though it could evolve into a more efficient form of government not too unlike our own. It might give an opportunity, I thought, for Tibetan officials to learn from Chinese officials about the methods of their administration, which, communism apart, was undeniably better organized than ours.

It was not long before these hopes were dead. All the worst I had seen in Chinese political meetings was repeated. I had not made enough allowance for one essential fact. Twenty of the members, although they were Tibetans, were representing the Chamdo Liberation Committee and the committee set up in the Panchen Lama's western district. These were both purely Chinese creations. Their representatives owed their positions mainly to Chinese support, and in return they had to support any Chinese proposition; though the Chamdo representatives did behave more reasonably than the Panchen Lama's. With this solid block of controlled votes, in addition to those of the five Chinese members, the Committee was powerless—a mere façade of Tibetan representation behind which all the effective power was exercised by the Chinese. In fact, all basic policy was decided by another body called the Committee of the Chinese Communist Party in Tibet, which had no Tibetan members. We were allowed to discuss the minor points, but we could never make any major changes. Although I was nominally chairman, there was nothing much I could do. Sometimes it was almost laughable to see how the proceedings were controlled and regulated, so that plans already completed in the other committee received a pointless and empty discussion and then were passed. But often I felt embarrassed at these meetings. I saw that the Chinese had only made me chairman in order to give an added appearance of Tibetan authority to their schemes.

As soon as the Committee began to set up its departments of government, the people began to learn what was happening, and their reaction was not surprising. All their old hostility to everything Chinese was reawakened. In Lhasa, a public meeting was held to protest against this new organization, and a resolution was drafted and sent to the Chinese authorities. It said that Tibet had had its own system of administration for a very long time, and therefore the new organization was unnecessary and ought to be abolished. Of course, the Chinese did not reply to that, although it was a popular demand. They summoned the Cabinet and said that as the Cabinet had not succeeded in banning public meetings, they would now approach me to do so. So the Cabinet unwillingly drafted a new proclamation, which I unwillingly signed, knowing quite well that suppressing public meetings would not suppress public opinion. Inevitably, popular indignation broke out in another way.

It happened during the Monlam Festival at the beginning of 1956. The resentment of the ordinary people against the Chinese had created something totally new in Tibet: political leaders spontaneously chosen by the people. These men were not government officials. They had no official standing at all, but came from all ordinary walks of life. And when I describe them as political leaders, I do not mean that they were political in any Western sense. They were not opposed to the Chinese because they were Communist; they had nothing to do with the political theories which divide the world. They were simply men who shared the misery and rage of our inarticulate people, and happened to have the native ability to put it into words and actions. So they rose to positions of influence.

These were the men who organized and led the Lhasan population. On the whole, the anger they felt and expressed on behalf of the people had its normal human reaction— they wanted to hit back. And inevitably that brought them into conflict sometimes with my Cabinet, who saw as I did the futility of trying to hit back against the Chinese army. The Cabinet had to restrain them from a policy which was patriotic but suicidal. On the other hand, they naturally thought the Cabinet went too far in appeasing the invaders. Sometimes I had to intervene and oppose their violent instincts for the sake of the very people they represented. They might have resented that, but to the bitter end they remained passionately loyal to me. I do not flatter myself that I earned this loyalty by personal qualities of my own. It was the concept of the Dalai Lama which held their loyalty, as it did and does of all Tibetans. I was the symbol of what they were fighting for.

For my part, I admired them even while I had to oppose them. I was glad our misfortune had shown that such qualities of leadership existed among Tibetans. They are qualities we shall always need.

The activities of these leaders during the Monlam Festival were a strange contrast with the time-honored celebrations. For the first time, the Festival had political overtones, and nobody could help being aware of them. While the processions circulated and the monks thronged in the streets, pamphlets were being stuck up all over the city. As usual, they demanded that the Chinese must go, and leave Tibet to the Tibetans. As usual, this incensed the Chinese generals, and as usual they sent for the Cabinet and put the blame on them. But this time, among their angry threats, they also named three of the popular leaders. They were among the men who had issued the resolution against the Preparatory Committee; and the Chinese insisted they were also responsible for the pamphlets and posters, and demanded that the Cabinet should give orders for their arrest. They had broken no law of ours, but the Chinese threatened that if the Tibetans refused to arrest them, they would arrest them and interrogate them themselves. So, to save them from this much worse fate, the Cabinet had them put in prison. One died there, but the others were soon released when the three great monasteries of Lhasa stood surety for their behavior, and one of these men is with me now in India.

Meanwhile, such news as we had from Chamdo, the eastern district which was still entirely under Chinese military rule, showed that things there were getting worse and worse. During the Monlam Festival, fighting broke out in Litang beyond the boundary. Soon after the Preparatory Committee was inaugurated, the Chinese general in command in Chamdo called a meeting of about 350 leading Tibetan personalities. He told them that I had said Tibet was not ready for Communist reforms, and that they should only be introduced gradually, and not before a majority of Tibetans had approved them. But the Panchen Lama, he said, had demanded that they should be introduced at once. The meeting was to discuss these two alternatives and decide which of them should be accepted in Chamdo.

The discussions went on for days. At the end, about a hundred people voted to have the reforms when I and the rest of Tibet accepted them. About forty voted to have them straight away. The rest, roughly 200, voted never to have the reforms at all, although that had not been offered as an alternative. The general thanked them all, announced that the reforms would be introduced in due course, and presented each of the members with a picture book, a pen, ink and paper, and some toilet articles—which seemed curiously chosen gifts—and dismissed them.

Within a month, the officials of the border provinces were summoned again, this time to a fort called Jomdha Dzong, a district of Chamdo. They were surrounded by Chinese troops and told that "democratic" reforms would begin at once. They protested that they had seen the miseries democratic reforms had caused in the provinces just across the border, and they would have none of them. The Chinese kept them under constant persuasion in the fort for nearly a fortnight. By then, the officials had all given verbal agreement. They were told they would all be sent back to their districts to explain the reforms to the people, but first they must be given a course of instruction themselves.

Upon this agreement, the Chinese guards surrounding the fort relaxed, and in the night before the course of indoctrination was due to start, every one of the officials, over two hundred in number, broke out of the fort and took to the mountains.

So, by this senseless action, the Chinese had driven most of the leading men of the district into the life of guerrillas, outlaws who knew they would be arrested if they ever went back to their homes. They formed a nucleus which grew and was bound to go on growing. They had to depend for their defense on such arms and ammunition as they could capture from the Chinese; so they had to fight, whether it was their inclination or not. Those eastern Tibetans, the Khampas in particular, are tough and resolute people. They knew their mountains, and the mountains were ideal for guerrilla warfare. Already in the first half of 1956, there were stories of their raids on Chinese roads and depots.

This seemed to me to be a desperate situation without any imaginable end. In those impregnable mountains, the guerrillas could hold out for years. The Chinese would never be able to dislodge them. Yet they would never be able to defeat the Chinese army. And however long it went on, it would be the Tibetan people, especially the women and the children, who would suffer.

I was very despondent. The situation now had become even worse than it had been two years before. The vicious circle of dictatorial repression and popular resentment, which I thought I had broken when I allowed Lukhangwa to resign, had enclosed us again. So far, all my attempts at a peaceful solution of our problems had come to nothing, and with the Preparatory Committee a mere mockery of responsible government I could see no better hope of success in the future. Worst of all, I felt I was losing control of my own people. In the east they were being driven into barbarism. In central Tibet they were growing more determined to resort to violence; and I felt I would not be able to stop them much longer, even though I could not approve of violence and did not believe it could possibly help us.

My dual position as Dalai Lama, by which Tibet had been happily ruled for centuries, was becoming almost insupportable. In both my capacities as religious and secular leader, I felt bound to oppose any violence by the people. I knew the Chinese were trying to undermine my political authority; and in so far as I opposed the people's violent instincts, I was helping the Chinese to destroy the people's trust in me. Yet even if the people lost faith in me as their secular leader, they must not lose faith in me as religious leader, which was much more important. I could delegate or abdicate my secular leadership, but the Dalai Lama could never abdicate as religious leader, nor would I ever have dreamed of doing so.

Thus I began to think it might be in the best interests of Tibet if I withdrew from all political activities, in order to keep my religious authority intact. Yet while I was in Tibet, I could not escape from politics. To withdraw, I would have to leave the country, bitterly and desperately though I hated that idea.

At that moment of the depth of my despondency, I received an invitation to visit India.

8

A PILGRIMAGE TO INDIA

My friend the Maharaj Kumar of Sikkim had come to Lhasa especially to bring me the invitation, and his visit was like a ray of sympathy and sanity from the outside world. I was invited by the Mahabodhi Society of India, which is an institution founded seventy years ago to spread the teaching of Lord Buddha and to care for pilgrims and shrines in India. They asked me to come to attend the Buddha Jayanti, the two thousand five hundredth anniversary of the birth of Lord Buddha.

For every reason, political and religious, I very much wanted to go. The Buddha Jayanti itself would be an occasion of immense significance to all Buddhists. Besides, every Tibetan hoped to be able to go one day on a pilgrimage to India. For us, it had always been the Holy Land. It was the birthplace of the founder of Buddhist culture and the source of the wisdom brought to our mountains hundreds of years ago by Indian saints and seers. The religions and societies of Tibet and India had developed on different lines, but Tibet was still a child of Indian civilization.

And from the secular point of view, a visit to India seemed to offer me the very opportunity I wanted to withdraw from my close contact and fruitless arguments with the Chinese, at least for a time. Not only that—I hoped it would also give me a chance to ask Mr. Nehru and other democratic leaders and followers of Mahatma Gandhi for advice. I cannot exaggerate our feeling of political solitude in Tibet. I knew I was still inexperienced in international politics, but so was everyone else in our country. We knew other countries had faced situations like ours, and that a great fund of political wisdom and experience existed in the democratic world; but so far, none of it had been available to us, and we had had to act by a kind of untrained instinct. We desperately wanted sympathetic wise advice.

There was yet another reason why I wanted to go. For a long time, we had had friendly contacts with the British government of India. In fact, that had been our only contact with the Western world. But since the transfer of power in India to the Indian government, the political contact with India had faded away, and I was sure that we must try to renew it and keep it strong, as a life-line to the world of tolerance and freedom.

It was not only my own wish that I should go. The people of Tibet came to know of the invitation, and through my officials they pressed me to accept it, for all the reasons I have mentioned—except that it had not occurred to them, as it had to me, that I ought to withdraw from the immediate problems of politics.

But merely to want to go was not enough. If the Chinese did not want me to go, they could easily stop me, and so I had to begin by asking for their approval.

I consulted General Fan Ming, who had been in Lhasa from the beginning and was acting at the time as the senior Chinese government representative. He started by saying that he could only offer me suggestions; but he did not really leave me any doubt that they would be the kind of suggestions which have to be accepted, and my heart sank as he spoke. For reasons of security, he said, a visit to India was undesirable. He also thought that as the Preparatory Committee still had so much work to do, and as I was its chairman, I ought to stay in Lhasa. And then he added, like a consolation, that after all the invitation had only come from a religious organization, not from the government of India, so that there was no need for me to accept it, and I could easily send a deputy.

I was very disappointed, but I could not bring myself to give up my hope entirely, so I put off naming a deputy, and did not tell the Mahabodhi Society that I could not come. Four months later, about the middle of October 1956, the General suggested again that I should name a deputy, because the name had to be sent in advance to India; and then I did arrange for a delegation headed by my Junior Tutor to go on my behalf. But on the first or second of November, he came to see me again, and admitted that on the first of October the Chinese government had had a telegram from the Indian government inviting me and the Panchen Lama as its guests for the celebration. And he added that the Chinese government had considered the matter in all its aspects, and it would be all right for me to go if I wanted to. I was delighted, and so were the Lhasan people. And the story went round that the Indian Consul General in Lhasa had told several people about the invitation before General Fan Ming told me; and of course everyone inferred that the Chinese had been trying to keep the invitation secret until it was too late for me to accept it, and had only been forced to make up their minds by this disclosure.

So I prepared to go. But before I left Lhasa, I was given a long lecture, as if I were a schoolboy, by General Chang Chin-wu, who had just returned as the permanent representative of China. I found it very interesting, though perhaps not in quite the way that he intended. He said that recently there had been a little trouble in Hungary and Poland. It had been engineered by small groups of people under the influence of foreign imperialists, but Soviet Russia had immediately responded to the Hungarian and Polish people's call for help, and had put down the reactionaries without any difficulty. Reactionaries were always looking out for chances to create trouble in socialist countries, but the solidarity of the socialist powers was so great that they would always go to the help of any of these countries. He talked about this so long that I realized it was the hint of a warning that no other country would be allowed to interfere in Tibet.

And then he went on to talk of my visit to India. Although the occasion of the Jayanti, he said, was purely religious, it had something to do with UNESCO. The Chinese government was sending a delegation to it, but there was a possibility the Kuomintang would also try to send one from Formosa. If they did, the Chinese would leave the meeting, and they had already told the Indian government so; and I was also to refuse to take part if anyone from Formosa was present. The Chinese Ambassador would give me the latest information as soon as I reached India.

Next he warned me that if any of the Indian leaders asked me about the Indo-Tibetan frontier, I was only to say that this was a matter for the Foreign Office in Peking. I might also be asked, he said, about the situation in Tibet. If newspapermen or junior officials asked me, I was to say that there had been a little trouble, but everything was normal now. If it was Mr. Nehru or other high officials of the Indian government who asked, I could tell them a little more— that there had been uprisings in some parts of Tibet.

The final part of this lecture was a suggestion that if I was likely to have to make speeches during the celebration, I had better prepare them in advance in Lhasa. I was in fact expecting to make a speech at the Buddha Jayanti, and before I left Lhasa a draft was written for me by Ngabo, as

Secretary-General of the Preparatory Committee, in consultation with the Chinese. I rewrote it entirely after I came to India.

By then, a road had been built as far as Yatung, which was only two days' march from the frontier. It was part of a network of strategic roads which the Chinese were feverishly building so that they could cover our country with their military posts; but it had also shortened the journey from Lhasa to India from a matter of weeks to a matter of only days. We drove to Yatung in two days. On the way, at Shigatse, where the Chinese had put a car ferry across the Brahmaputra River, the Panchen Lama joined us. On the fourth day, we took to ponies, which were still the only means of crossing the Himalayan passes.

A Chinese general called Thin Ming-yi, a deputy divisional commander, came with us as far as Chumbithang, the last settlement in Tibet; and when he left us there he gave me another little lecture. There were many reactionaries in India, he said regretfully, and I must be very careful if I had to talk to them. He reminded me that as a vice-chairman of the Chinese National Assembly I was representing China as well as Tibet. So I must tell everyone of the great progress China had made in developing natural resources and raising the living standards of the people. I must not leave any doubt in the minds of the people I met that there was complete religious freedom, and every other kind of freedom, in China and Tibet. And if anyone did not believe me, I could tell them they were welcome to visit China whenever they liked.

That was the last installment of advice I was given before I crossed the border.

The descent from Tibet to India is a dramatic journey. For fifty miles across the desolate Tibetan plateau, the white peak of Chomolhari leads one on. At Phari, one passes close to the base of the mountain, and sees in full its isolated splendor. Then the track falls abruptly, down and down into the pine and rhododendron forests of the Chumbi Valley, where delphiniums and aconites and yellow poppies grow profusely; and one has a sense of climbing down to a totally different world, of the vast hot plains of India stretching far below and far ahead, and of the teeming cities and the oceans which few Tibetans have ever seen. But there is still a pass to climb, the Nathu-la, and the track leads up again above the forest line to the frontier at the top, and takes one back again to the familiar barren scenery of Tibet before it finally descends to the valleys of Sikkim.

The route through the Chumbi Valley has always been the main gateway between Tibet and India. It was the route which the British expedition followed in 1903, and the route which traders used after the agreement of 1904, as far as Gyantse—the only route on which any foreigners had rights in Tibet. In the valley is the town of Yatung, to which I had moved when the Chinese invasion had started in 1950. But it had changed since then. Then, I rode down to the valley on a pony; now, I drove down on the Chinese road in a Chinese car. It was certainly ten times faster and more convenient, but like all Tibetans, I preferred it as it had always been before. And incidentally, on the top of that road, near Phari, there was an example of how ridiculous the Chinese could sometimes look. I suppose they had read of the rarified atmosphere of the high mountains; for there on the road where people had traveled for centuries on foot and on horseback, one could now see Chinese driving comfortably in their cars, wearing oxygen masks.

Beyond Yatung, the scenery was new to me, and after leaving the car I rode up towards the frontier on the Nathu-la, free for the moment from my Chinese supervisors, with a feeling of pleasant anticipation and excitement I had not experienced since I was a boy. When we started the long climb, the weather was bright and clear, but we soon rode up into cloud, and the last few thousand feet were damp and cold. That only gave added pleasure to the warmth of our welcome at the top. The first thing I saw at the frontier was a guard of honor; then I was being greeted by the Maharaj Kumar and the Indian political officer in Sikkim, who also brought me the greetings of the President, Vice President, Prime Minister, and government of India. He presented a scarf to me, the symbol of greeting in Tibet, and a garland of flowers, the corresponding traditional symbol in India. We rode down the pass in company, and spent a happy night at Tsongo on the Sikkimese side.

Next day we left for Gangtok, the capital of Sikkim. As we went on through Sikkim and northern India, changing our transport stage by stage from the archaic to the modern, the spontaneous happy welcome grew, and I almost felt as if I were not in a foreign country at all; I felt at home. At the tenth mile we left our ponies and took to jeeps, and there the Chinese ambassador joined the party. Then, a little way out of the town, the Maharajah of Sikkim and his ministers joined us, and I changed from the jeep to his car. There was rather a comic incident with that car. It was flying a Sikkimese flag on one side and a Tibetan flag on the other. But we stopped for a little while on the way into the town. A great crowd of people was throwing scarves and flowers in greeting, when I was surprised to see a solitary Chinese gentleman, who turned out to be the Ambassador's interpreter, furtively removing the Tibetan flag and tying on a Chinese flag instead. My Indian friends noticed him too, and I was delighted to find that they also saw the funny side of it.

We ended the journey in a special plane, and as we approached New Delhi I had a marvelous view of the capital which the British built and then left as a legacy to the new and free India. At the airport, the Vice President, Dr. Radhakrishnan, and the Prime Minister, Mr. Nehru, were waiting to welcome me. The Chinese Ambassador, who was in the plane with me, insisted on introducing me, first to them and then to the members of the diplomatic corps. He took me along the line, presenting the officials of many countries. We came to the representative of Britain; but what was going to happen, I wondered, when we came to the representative of the United States? It was a delicate exercise in diplomatic manners. At the crucial moment, the Chinese Ambassador suddenly vanished like a magician, and I was left face-to-face with the American. Somebody from the Indian Foreign Office tactfully stepped in and introduced us.

I drove into the city with Dr. Radhakrishnan, and he told me how glad he was to meet me and spoke charmingly of the long connections between our countries. Big crowds had gathered on the roadsides to add to my welcome, under the flags and decorations put up for the Buddha Jayanti. We went to the Rashtrapati Bhavan, the President's official residence, and there the President, Dr. Rajendra Prasad, received me with his gentle smile and voice on the threshold of the Durbar room. I was greatly and happily impressed by both these leaders. I felt they were devout and learned men who symbolized the eternal spirit of the Indian people.

My very first visit on my first morning in New Delhi was to the Rajghat, the place of cremation of Mahatma Gandhi. I was deeply moved as I prayed there on the green lawns which slope down to the Jamuna River. I felt I was in the presence of a noble soul—the soul of the man who in his life was perhaps the greatest of our age, the man who had contended till death itself to preserve the spirit of India and mankind—a true disciple of Lord Buddha and a true believer in peace and harmony among all men. As I stood there I wondered what wise counsel the Mahatma would have given me if he had been alive. I felt sure he would have thrown all his strength of will and character into a peaceful campaign for the freedom of the people of Tibet.

I wished most fervently that I had had the privilege of meeting him in this world. But, standing there, I felt I had come in close touch with him, and I felt his advice would always be that I should follow the path of peace. I had and still have unshaken faith in the doctrine of nonviolence which he preached and practiced. Now I made up my mind more firmly to follow his lead whatever difficulties might confront me. I determined more strongly than ever that I could never associate myself with acts of violence.

After that pilgrimage, I was busy for two or three days with the celebrations of the Buddha Jayanti. It gave me just the opportunity I wanted so much to talk to wise men from different parts of the world who were working, free from any immediate oppression, to proclaim the teaching of Lord Buddha for the sake of the peace of the world. Peace between nations was the uppermost thought in my own mind; so when I gave an address at the symposium, I emphasized the peaceful nature of the Buddhist faith. I said I hoped these celebrations would help to spread the knowledge of the path of enlightenment not only in Asia but also among the people of the western world; for the teaching of Lord Buddha could lead not only to contented and peaceful lives for individuals, but also to an end of hostility between nations. The salvation of humanity could be found in the principles of Buddhism. And I may add now that I would gladly extend this statement. The salvation of humanity lies in the religious instinct latent in all men, whatever their creed. It is the forcible repression of this instinct which is the enemy of peace.

It was after these celebrations that I had my first real talk with Mr. Nehru, and by then my opinions had evolved to a further stage. I have explained already why I had wanted to come to India; now I had reluctantly come to a new conclusion. I believed I ought not to go home again; I believed I ought to stay in India until there was some positive sign of a change in Chinese policy. Perhaps my feeling of the closeness of Mahatma Gandhi, and my meetings with so many learned sympathetic men, had helped to bring me to this sad decision. For almost the first time, I had met people who were not Tibetans but felt true sympathy for Tibet. At home, I thought, I could not help my people any more;

I could not control their wish to resort to violence; all my peaceful efforts so far had been failures. But from India, I could at least tell people all over the world what was happening in Tibet, and try to mobilize their moral support for us, and so perhaps bring a change in China's ruthless policy.

I had to explain this to Mr. Nehru. We met alone, except for his Tibetan interpreter. I told him first how grateful I was for the chance to visit India and come to the Buddha Jayanti. And then I explained how desperate things had become in eastern Tibet, and how we all feared that worse troubles would spread through the rest of the country. I said I was forced to believe that the Chinese really meant to destroy our religion and customs for ever, and so cut off our historic ties with India. And all Tibetans, I told him, now pinned their remaining hopes on the government and people of India. And then I explained why I wanted to stay in India until we could win back our freedom by peaceful means.

He was very kind and listened patiently, but he was firmly convinced that nothing could be done for Tibet at present. He said that nobody had ever formally recognized our country's independence. He agreed with me that it was useless to try to fight against the Chinese. If we tried, they could easily bring in more forces to crush us completely. And he advised me to go back to Tibet and work peacefully to try to carry out the Seventeen-Point Agreement.

I said I had done all I possibly could to carry it out, but however hard I tried, the Chinese refused to honor their side of the agreement, and I could not see any sign of a change of heart among them. At that, he promised to speak to Chou En-lai, who was coming to India on the following day, and our interview ended.

I also spoke to Chou En-lai. I went to the airport to meet him, and the same evening I had a long talk with him. I told him that in our eastern provinces the situation was getting worse and worse. The Chinese were enforcing changes without any thought for local conditions or the wishes or interests of the people. Chou En-lai seemed sympathetic, and said the local Chinese officials must have been making mistakes. He said he would report what I had said to Mao Tsetung, but I could not tie him down to any definite promise of improvement.

But a few days later, Chou En-lai invited my elder brothers Thubten Norbu and Gyelo Thondup to dinner at the Chinese embassy, and the conversation they had with him was rather more hopeful and specific. My brothers had no official position in our government, and so they could afford to speak more frankly without fear of direct repercussions in Tibet; and when they told me of their conversation afterwards, it seemed that they had been thoroughly outspoken in their criticisms. They told Chou En-lai that for centuries Tibet had respected China as an important and friendly neighbor. Yet now the Chinese in Tibet were treating Tibetans as if they were deadly enemies. They were making deliberate use of the worst types of Tibetans, the misfits in Tibetan society, to stir up discord, and they were ignoring the many patriotic Tibetans who might have been able to improve relations between Tibetans and Chinese. They were supporting the Panchen Lama in secular matters, in order to reopen the old rift between his predecessor and mine, and so undermine the authority of our government. And they were keeping such vast unnecessary armies in Tibet, especially in Lhasa, that our economy was ruined and prices had risen to the point where Tibetans were facing starvation. It was not the ruling classes of Tibet but the mass of the people who were most bitter against the Chinese occupation. It was they who were demanding that the armies should withdraw and a new agreement, as between equal partners, should be signed; but the Chinese in Lhasa would not listen to popular opinion.

Chou En-lai did not seem to enjoy this plain-speaking,

but he remained as polite and suave as ever. He assured my brothers that the Chinese government had no thought of using undesirable Tibetans, or the Panchen Lama, to undermine my authority or cause dissension. They did not want to interfere in Tibet's affairs, or to be an economic burden. He agreed that perhaps some difficulties had been caused by lack of understanding among local Chinese officials; and he promised to improve the food supplies in Lhasa, and to begin gradual withdrawal of Chinese troops as soon as Tibet could manage her own affairs. And he also said he would report their complaints to Mao Tse-tung, and would see that the causes of them were removed. These promises were not mere words, he said; my brothers could stay in India if they liked, to see whether his promises were fulfilled, and if they were not, they would be perfectly free to criticize the Chinese government.

But at the end of the interview, he told them that he also had a request to make. He had heard that I had been thinking of staying in India, but he wanted them to persuade me to go back to Tibet. It could only harm me and my people, he said, if I did not go.

After those meetings with Chou En-lai, I started on a tour of parts of India. I was taken to several new industrial projects, such as the huge hydroelectric scheme at Nangal, and I saw for myself, for the first time, the great difference between the way that such things are organized under communism and under a free democracy—the whole difference of atmosphere and spirit between conscripted labor and voluntary labor. But my main object, of course, was to follow my pilgrimage to historic religious centers. So I went to Sanchi, Ajanta, Benares, and Budh Gaya. I was lost in admiration of masterpieces of Indian religious art, with their evidence both of creative genius and of fervent faith. I reflected how sectarianism and communal hatred had harmed this heritage in the past, and how hatred had been changed to calm and peace by the assurance of religious freedom in the Indian Constitution.

In Benares and Budh Gaya I found thousands of Tibetan pilgrims who were waiting to see me, and I spoke to them in both places on the doctrines of Lord Buddha, and impressed on them that they should always follow the path of peace which he clearly marked out for us.

My visit to Budh Gaya was a source of deep inspiration for me. Every devout Buddhist will always associate Budh Gaya with all that is noblest and loftiest in his religious and cultural inheritance. From my very early youth I had thought and dreamed about this visit. Now I stood in the presence of the Holy Spirit who had attained Mahaparinirvana, the highest Nirvana, in this sacred place, and had found for all mankind the path to salvation. As I stood there, a feeling of religious fervor filled my heart, and left me bewildered with the knowledge and impact of the divine power which is in all of us.

But while I was still on my pilgrimage, having traveled on to Sarnath, a messenger came to me from the Chinese embassy in Delhi. He brought a telegram from General Chang Chin-wu, the Chinese representative in Lhasa. It said the situation at home was serious; spies and collaborators were planning a huge revolt; I should return as soon as possible. And at Budh Gaya itself, one of my Chinese escorts gave me a message that Chou En-lai was coming back to Delhi and was anxious to see me. So after a few more days, I had to drag myself back to the world of politics, hostility and mistrust.

In Delhi, Chou En-lai told me again that the situation in Tibet was worse, and that I ought to go back. He left me in no doubt that if there really was a popular uprising he was ready to use force to put it down. I remember him saying that the Tibetans who were living in India were bent on making trouble, and that I must make up my mind what course I would take myself. I told him I was not ready yet to say what I would do, and I repeated all I had told him before of our grievances against the Chinese occupation. And I said we were willing to forget whatever wrongs had been done to us in the past, but the inhuman treatment and oppression must be stopped. He answered that Mao Tse-tung had made it perfectly clear that "reforms" would only be introduced in Tibet in accordance with the wishes of the people. He spoke as though he still could not understand why Tibetans did not welcome the Chinese.

He told me he had heard I had been invited to visit Kalimpong, in the north of India near the border of Tibet, where there was a community of Tibetans, some of whom had already been driven into exile by the Chinese rule. He said I ought not to go, in case the people there created trouble. I only told him I would think that over. And he ended our interview by warning me that some Indian officials were very good, but others were very peculiar, so that I must be careful. It was an inconclusive talk, and I came away feeling frustrated and dissatisfied.

The next morning another senior member of the Chinese government, Marshal Ho Lung, came to repeat Chou En-lai's advice that I should go back at once to Lhasa. I remember him quoting a Chinese proverb: "The snow lion looks dignified if he stays in his mountain abode, but if he comes down to the valleys he is treated like a dog." I was not disposed to argue any more. By then, I had thought over Mr. Nehru's advice, and the assurances which Chou En-lai had given to me and my brothers. I told the Marshal I had decided to return, and that I trusted the promises made to me and my brothers would be honored.

Before I left Delhi, I had a final interview with Mr. Nehru, and I think I should quote his own account of his meetings with Chou En-lai and with me. He gave the account to the Lower House of the Indian Parliament in 1959.

"When Premier Chou En-lai came here two or three years ago," he said, "he was good enough to discuss Tibet with me at considerable length. We had a frank and full talk. He told me that while Tibet had long been a part of the Chinese state, they did not consider Tibet as a province of China. The people were different from the people of China proper, just as in other autonomous regions of the Chinese state the people were different, even though they formed part of that state. Therefore, they considered Tibet an autonomous region which would enjoy autonomy. He told me further that it was absurd for anyone to imagine that China was going to force communism on Tibet. Communism could not be enforced in this way on a very backward country, and they had no wish to do so, even though they would like reforms to come in progressively. Even these reforms they proposed to postpone for a considerable time."

And in speaking of his meetings with me, Mr. Nehru said: "About that time the Dalai Lama was also here, and I had long talks with him then. I told him of Premier Chou En-lai's friendly approach and of his assurance that he would respect the autonomy of Tibet. I suggested to him that he should accept these assurances in good faith and cooperate in maintaining that autonomy and bringing about certain reforms in Tibet. The Dalai Lama agreed that his country, though according to him advanced spiritually, was very backward socially and economically, and reforms were needed."

I remember telling Mr. Nehru in that final meeting that I had made up my mind to go back to Tibet for two reasons: because he had advised me to do so, and because Chou En-lai had given definite promises to me and my brothers.

Mr. Nehru's personality had impressed me very much. Although the mantle of Mahatma Gandhi had fallen on him, I could not catch any glimpse of spiritual fervor in him; but I saw him as a brilliant practical statesman, with a masterly grasp of international politics, and he showed me that he had a profound love for his country and faith in his people. For their welfare and progress, he was firm in the pursuit of peace.

I also remember that in that interview we talked about my wish to go to Kalimpong. Mr. Nehru knew that Chou En-lai had advised me not to go, and he seemed to agree that the people up there might be troublesome and might try to persuade me not to go back to Tibet. India was a free country, he said, and nobody could stop the people of Kalimpong expressing their own opinions. But he added that if I really wanted to go, his government would make all the arrangements and look after me.

I decided I ought to go, in spite of Chou En-lai's advice. It was not entirely a political matter. I had a spiritual duty to visit my countrymen, on which Chou En-lai could certainly not advise me.

So I went there, and met not only the Tibetans who were living there, but also a deputation which had been sent by my government in Lhasa to escort me home. And in fact, they all suggested that I should stay in India, because the situation in Tibet had become so desperate and dangerous. But I had made up my mind that one more chance must be given to the Chinese to carry out their government's promises, and one more effort must be made for freedom through peaceful means.

I was weary of politics. Political talks had taken up most of my time in Delhi, and cut short my pilgrimage. I had begun to detest them, and would gladly have retired from politics altogether if I had not had a duty to my people in Tibet. So I was happy to find that in Kalimpong and Gangtok I had time for meditation and for religious discourses to the people who had gathered there to hear me.

It was snowing hard in the mountains. I had to wait nearly a month before the way to Tibet, across the Nathu-la, was open.

▣ 9 ▣

REVOLT

At last the weather improved and the way was open. At the top of the Nathu-la I said good-by to the last of my friends from India and Sikkim. As I walked across the top of the pass, into Tibet, I saw that among the little prayer flags which Tibetans always like to fly in high places, enormous red flags of China had been hoisted, and portraits of Mao Tse-tung. No doubt this was meant as a welcome, but it was a melancholy welcome to my own country.

A Chinese general was waiting to receive me. But luckily, it was General Chin Rhawo-rhen, a deputy divisional commander, and he was one of the Chinese officers I really liked. He was a sincere, straightforward man; not the only one by any means—I had met others who were equally honest and sympathetic. I am perfectly certain that many of them would have liked to help us, but they were all subject to strict Communist discipline, and there was very little they could do. One of them, however, felt so strongly that he joined our guerrilla forces in 1958 and fought with them for nine months, and is now a refugee in India.

I had decided that on my way back to Lhasa I would speak freely in the towns we passed through—Yatung, Gyantse, and Shigatse. After the promises my brothers and I had been given in Delhi, I wanted to see what the Chinese reaction would be to a little plain-speaking in Tibet. So in my speeches at all these three places, and in Lhasa too, I repeated emphatically what I had always told my people, and the Chinese and Tibetan officials, since my return from China in 1955: that the Chinese were not our rulers, and we were not their subjects. We had been promised autonomous government, and everyone should do his best to make it work. Our duty should always be to right wrongs, whether they were committed by Chinese or by Tibetans. The rulers of China had assured me, I said, that the Chinese were only in Tibet to help the Tibetans, and therefore any Chinese who failed to be helpful to us was disobeying his own central government.

I put this policy into practice also, by seeing that every action of our government was strictly in accordance with the Seventeen-Point Agreement, and by pressing in every way I could toward autonomy. At first, I could see no reaction from the Chinese, but slowly I began to understand that they simply thought I was acting under foreign influences.

I soon learned that all the time I had been in India, the anger of the people against the Chinese had been rising steadily, both in Lhasa and in the outlying districts. The main reason for this, I think, was that Khampas and other refugees from the eastern provinces had been streaming westward. There were thousands of them already camped round Lhasa for the protection of the government. Everybody had learned from them of the atrocious methods the Chinese were using in the east to try to enforce their doctrines, and all were afraid that the same methods would soon be used in the rest of Tibet.

But while the temper of the people was steadily building up toward revolt, the attitude of the Chinese authorities varied in the most extraordinary and disconcerting way. Just before I came home, there was a period in which they were as courteous to my ministers as only Chinese can be. In that period, they called a meeting and told the Cabinet that the Chinese government understood that the people were getting anxious about the proposals for reform in Tibet. They did not in the least want to disregard the people's wishes, and so the reforms would be postponed for six years. I do not know whether this was a result of my protests to Chou En-lai in Delhi; whether it was or not, it came too late to have much effect on the people's hostility.

In the same period of studied friendliness, however, the Chinese announced at a public meeting—without having warned the Cabinet—that revolt had broken out in the east against their rule, and that they were fully prepared to do whatever was needed to crush it. This was a shock to the ministers. They had known, of course, that the Khampas were fighting, but they had not known that the revolt was serious enough to make the Chinese admit its existence in public.

And then suddenly, without any immediate reason that we could see, the friendly period came to an end, and we were back again in the old atmosphere of threats, demands, and scarcely veiled abuse.

After my visit to India, I had invited Mr. Nehru to come to Lhasa. I did this not only because I would have liked to entertain him there, to show my gratitude for the hospitality I had received in India, but also, of course, because I wanted him to have a firsthand impression of what was happening in Tibet. He accepted, and the Chinese made no objection at first. But I might have known what would happen. I might have known that they would not dare to allow a statesman from the outside world to see what they were doing. Shortly before the visit was due, they explained that they could not guarantee his safety in Tibet—suggesting that the Tibetans might have harmed him, instead of welcoming him, as they certainly would have, as a savior—so that unfortunately my invitation would have to be withdrawn. So I was to be cut off again from all sympathy and advice.

Slowly, from the reports of refugees, we began to receive a clearer impression of the terrible things that were happening in the east and northeast, though the exact history of them is not known to this day, and possibly never will be. There, in the district which had been entirely under Chinese rule since the invasion began, the number of Khampas who had taken to the mountains as guerrillas had grown from hundreds to tens of thousands. They had already fought some considerable battles with the Chinese army. The Chinese were using artillery and bomber aircraft, not only against the guerrillas when they could find them, but also against the villages and monasteries whose people they suspected, rightly or wrongly, of having helped them. Thus villages and monasteries were being totally destroyed. Lamas and the lay leaders of the people were being humiliated, imprisoned, killed, and even tortured. Land was confiscated. Sacred images, books of scriptures, and other things of holy significance to us, were broken up, derided, or simply stolen. Blasphemous proclamations were made on posters and in newspapers and preached in schools, saying that religion was only a means of exploiting the people, and that Lord Buddha was a "reactionary." A few copies of these newspapers, which had been published in Chinese territory, reached Lhasa and began to circulate among Tibetan and Chinese officials there; and the Chinese, seeing the strong Tibetan reaction and realizing that they had gone too far, offered five dollars a copy for them, to try to take them out of circulation before everybody in Lhasa had heard of them.

If the Chinese had ever wanted to win over Tibetans as willing citizens of their "motherland," they had evidently given up the attempt, at least in the eastern provinces. Tibetans could never be awed or terrified into acquiescence, and to attack our religion, our most precious possession, was a lunatic policy. The effect of these actions was simply to spread and intensify the revolt. Within a short time after my return to Lhasa, people were taking to arms throughout the east, northeast, and southeast of Tibet. It was only the western and central parts of the country which were still in comparative peace.

Of course, I protested very strongly to the Chinese general in Lhasa against these shocking tactics. When I protested, for example, against the bombing of villages and monasteries, he would promise to put a stop to it at once, but it continued exactly the same.

In Lhasa, the number of Khampas, Amdo people, and other people from the east grew to at least ten thousand. Some of them were permanent residents, but most were refugees. As it was eastern people who had started the revolt, these people in Lhasa began to worry that the Chinese might take revenge on them, and they sent a petition to the Cabinet, asking for protection. The Chinese commanders told the Cabinet they could assure them that they would not take punitive action against eastern people in general, and the Cabinet sent for the local Khampa leaders and did their best to overcome their fears. But they only succeeded in calming them for a little while. They came back, and asked the Cabinet to get a formal assurance in writing from the Chinese that the Khampas and Amdo people would not be punished. But the Chinese refused to give that, on the curious ground that if such an assurance became public, it would reach India, and China would lose face.

There was nothing more the Cabinet could do, except repeat the verbal promise the Chinese had given, and put it in writing on their own authority. But there were soon signs that this promise might be as empty as so many others. Within a few weeks, Chinese officers began to go round the tents of the Khampas taking a census, and writing down all kinds of details of the personal history of everyone they found there. This was something they had never done before, and it aroused fresh fears in the Khampas' minds. They thought it was the prelude to mass arrests, and they decided they were not safe in Lhasa any longer. So a great exodus began. Group after group of the refugees set off for the mountains by night, some taking their families with them, to find the guerrilla bands and join them, until hardly any were left.

Of course, this made the Chinese angry, and their complaints poured into the Cabinet office. I was very unhappy too at this turn of events. It made my dilemma even more acute. Part of me greatly admired the guerrilla fighters. They were brave people, men and women, and they were putting their lives and their children's lives at stake to try to save our religion and country in the only remaining way that they could see. When one heard of the terrible deeds of the Chinese in the east, it was a natural human reaction to seek revenge. And moreover, I knew they regarded themselves as fighting in loyalty to me as Dalai Lama: the Dalai Lama was the core of what they were trying to defend.

Yet I was forced back to my old argument. I often thought again of my visit to the Rajghat, and wondered afresh what advice Mahatma Gandhi would have given me in the changing circumstances. Would he still have advised nonviolence? I could only believe he would. However great the violence used against us, it could never become right to use violence in reply. And on the practical side, I saw the atrocities in the east as a dreadful example of what the Chinese could do so easily all over Tibet if we fought them. I must, I thought, try yet again to persuade my people not to use arms, not to provoke the same or worse reprisals over the rest of our country. I asked the Cabinet to send a message to the Khampa leaders that these were my wishes. They appointed a mission of two lay officials and three monks to find the guerrilla leaders and tell them. The same mission took a promise from the Chinese that if the guerrillas laid down their arms, no action would be taken against them. That promise carried the implication that if they refused, action would be severe. The Chinese had wanted to demand, in return for their promise, that the Khampas should actually surrender their arms, but the Cabinet persuaded them not to make that demand, because they knew that no Khampa would ever accept it.

During this time, I had several talks with the three senior generals, Chang Chin-wu, Tan Kuo-hwa, and Tan Kuan-sen. What they said hardly seemed to bear any relation to what was happening. Every time I met them, they repeated the assurances that Chou En-lai had given me in India: no drastic changes would be made in Tibet for at least six years, and even after that they would not be enforced against the wishes of the people. Yet they were already enforcing them, against the very emphatic wishes of the people, in the eastern districts. Perhaps they were able to persuade themselves that these districts were part of China itself, not of Tibet. But their repeated promise gave me a last straw of hope to cling to, which was perhaps what they intended.

Then they suddenly changed their policy. Hitherto, it was they, the Chinese army, who had taken reprisals against the guerrillas in the east, and threatened them elsewhere. Now they insisted that our government should take action against them. We should send our own Tibetan army to crush the revolt. They would provide us with reinforcements and supplies. But this the Cabinet absolutely rejected. They pointed out that the Tibetan army was much too small and not well enough trained or equipped, and that it was needed to keep the peace in Lhasa; and above all, they said they could not possibly guarantee that the Tibetan army would not simply join hands with the guerrillas. And I have no doubt that would have happened. It was unthinkable to send out a Tibetan army to fight against Tibetans who were committing no worse crime than to defend Tibet. So at last the Cabinet was forced into firm defiance of a major Chinese order.

The Chinese had an extraordinary way of mixing trivial demands with those of the highest importance. In the midst of all these desperate affairs, they insisted that the word "reactionaries" should always be used to describe the Khampas who had taken arms against them. The word has a special emotional significance for Communists, but of course it had none for us. Everybody, in the government and out, began to use it as a synonym for guerrillas. To Communists, no doubt, it implied the height of wickedness, but we used it, on the whole, in admiration. It did not seem to matter to us, or to the Khampas, what their fellow-Tibetans called them; but later, when I innocently used the word in writing, it did cause confusion among our friends abroad.

The Chinese showed the same lack of logic and balance in much more serious matters. The revolt had broken out in the district they themselves had controlled for seven years; yet now they furiously blamed our government for it. Their complaints and accusations were endless, day after day: the Cabinet was not trying to suppress the "reactionaries," it was leaving Tibetan armories unguarded, so that "reactionaries" could steal arms and ammunition. Consequently, hundreds of Chinese were losing their lives, and the Chinese would take vengeance in blood for them. Like all invaders, they had totally lost sight of the sole cause of the revolt against them: that our people did not want them in our country, and were ready to give their lives to be rid of them.

Yet while the Chinese blamed our government, they were still haunted by a specter of nonexistent "imperialists." They must have known by then that there were no "imperialist forces" in Tibet, and never had been, but now they said certain Tibetans in India had joined with the "imperialists," and it was they who were creating the trouble in Tibet. They named nine of them, including my former Prime Minister Lukhangwa and my brothers Thubten Norbu and Gyelo Thondup, and demanded that they should be deprived of their Tibetan nationality. This order did not seem to me, or to the Cabinet, to be worth defying. The accusation was nonsense, but these nine people might well have thought it an honor to be singled out in such a way, and the punishment, so far as I have heard, never caused them the slightest inconvenience.

But in Lhasa we had reached the breaking point. The breach between the Chinese and the Cabinet was already open. The Chinese were arming their civilians and reinforcing their barricades in the city. They declared that throughout the country they would only protect their own nationals and their own communications: everything else was our responsibility. They summoned more meetings in schools and other places, and told people that the Cabinet was in league with the "reactionaries" and its members would be dealt with accordingly—not merely shot, they sometimes went on to explain, but executed slowly and publicly. General Tan Kuan-sen, addressing a women's meeting in Lhasa, said that where there was rotten meat, the flies gathered, but if you got rid of the meat, the flies were no more trouble. The flies, I suppose, were the guerrilla fighters: the rotten meat was either my Cabinet or myself.

And yet, while the Chinese said the Cabinet was in league with the Khampa guerrillas, I have no doubt the Khampas believed the Cabinet was more or less in league with the Chinese. The mission which the Cabinet had sent to the Khampa leaders never came back. Its five members joined the guerrillas themselves, and by then it was very difficult to blame them. The wishes I had expressed through them caused a lull in the fighting, but they had come too late. Most of the guerrillas would not go back to their homes, because they did not trust the assurances that no action would be taken against them; and in fact, by then, a great many of them had no homes to go to.

I must admit I was very near despair. And then, either by accident or design, the Chinese brought the final crisis on us.

▣ 10 ▣

CRISIS IN LHASA

On the first of March, 1959, I was in the Jokhang, the main temple of Lhasa, for the celebrations of the Monlam Festival. It was during that festival that I took my final examination as Master of Metaphysics. Of course, through all our political misfortunes, my religious education had been continuing. It was still my greatest interest. All my own inclination would have been to pursue religious studies in peace, if that had been possible. The examination by dialectical debate before a vast audience of monks and lamas, which I have described already, was a tremendously important occasion for me, and indeed for the whole of Tibet, and I was entirely preoccupied at that moment with religious questions.

In the middle of all the ceremonies and preparations for my final test, I was told that two Chinese officers wanted to see me. They were shown in—two junior officers who said they had been sent by General Tan Kuan-sen. They wanted me to tell the general a date on which I could attend a theatrical show he had decided to stage in the Chinese army camp. I had already heard of this plan and had promised to go, but I really could not concentrate on anything else just then, so I told the officers I would arrange a date as soon as the ceremonies were finished in ten days' time. They would not be satisfied with that, but kept on pressing me to decide on a date at once. I repeated that I could only fix the date when the ceremonies were over, and finally they agreed to take that reply to the general.

This visit was curious. Normally, unless the general called on me himself, messages from him were sent through whichever of my officials were most concerned. Invitations to social functions were normally sent through Donyerchemo Phala, my Senior Chamberlain, or Chikyab Khempo, the Chief Official Abbot, and my representative in the Cabinet.

So the unusual procedure of sending junior officers to see me personally, and of sending them to the temple, immediately aroused suspicion among all my people who came to know of it. Apart from the resentment it understandably created among my officials, everyone felt the general was once again trying to lower the Dalai Lama in the eyes of his people.

It had been our painful experience under the Chinese regime that I did not have the option even to decline a social invitation if it did not suit me, except at the risk of incurring the displeasure of the Chinese and causing unpleasant repercussions. Their annoyance in such a case always found vent in some other direction, and so we thought it wiser, in the interest of the country, to suffer such minor humiliations in silence, rather than risk a further stiffening of the general Chinese policy of relegating me and my government to a position of subordination.

Nothing more was heard of this strange invitation before I left the temple for the Norbulingka on the fifth of March. My procession to the Norbulingka had always been a great occasion, and in previous years the Chinese had taken part in it, but this year everybody noticed that no Chinese attended.

It was two days later, on the seventh of March, that I had another message from the general. His interpreter, whose name was Li, telephoned to the Chief Official Abbot and asked for a definite date when I could attend the performance in the Chinese camp. The Abbot consulted me, and at my instance he told Li that the tenth of March would be convenient.

The arrangements to be made for my visit were not discussed until the ninth of March, the day before it was due. Then, at eight o'clock in the morning, two Chinese officers came to the house of the Commander of my Bodyguard, Kusung Depon, and told him they had been sent to take him to the Chinese headquarters to see Brigadier Fu, whose title was Military Advisor. Kusung Depon had not had his breakfast, and told them he would come at ten o'clock. They went away, but came back an hour later to tell him he must come at once, as the brigadier was waiting impatiently.

Later that morning, Kusung Depon came back to the Norbulingka in a state of distress. He spoke to my Chief Official Abbot and Senior Chamberlain, and they brought him to see me, and he gave me a verbatim account of what had happened.

The brigadier was looking angry, he told me, when he arrived at his office. "The Dalai Lama is coming here tomorrow," he said abruptly, "to see a dramatic show. There are some things to settle. That is why I have sent for you."

"Has the date been fixed?" Kusung Depon asked him.

"Don't you know?" snapped the brigadier. "The Dalai Lama has accepted the general's invitation and he is coming on the tenth. Now I want to make this clear to you: There will be none of the ceremony you usually have. None of your armed men are to come with him, as they do when he goes to the Preparatory Committee. No Tibetan soldier is to come beyond the Stone Bridge. If you insist, you may have two or three Tibetan bodyguards, but it is definitely decided that they must not be armed."

These unusual orders were a most unpleasant shock to my commander. The Stone Bridge was the limit of the vast army camp which contained the Chinese headquarters. The existence of this camp within two miles of the Norbulingka had always been an eyesore to every patriotic Tibetan. As long as the Chinese kept it to themselves, the people of Lhasa had tolerated it. But the very idea of the Dalai Lama going into it for any purpose was extraordinary, and Kusung Depon knew that the people would dislike it. If I had to go without a bodyguard, it was more extraordinary still. By custom, an escort of twenty-five armed guards accompanied the Dalai Lama wherever he went, and armed troops were always posted along the route. Kusung Depon knew that if this custom were to be suddenly stopped, an explanation would have to be given to the public. So he asked the brigadier for a reason. It was an innocent inquiry, but it further annoyed the brigadier.

"Will you be responsible if somebody pulls the trigger?" he shouted. "We don't want trouble. We shall have our own troops unarmed when the Dalai Lama comes. You can post your men on the road as far as the Stone Bridge if you like, but none of them are to come beyond it under any circumstances. And the whole thing is to be kept strictly secret."

There was much discussion among my officials when Kusung Depon returned and told us of these orders. There seemed to be no alternative but to comply with them, and plans for my visit were made accordingly.

But no one could help feeling that the whole of the Chinese invitation was suspicious, and their wish to keep the visit secret made the suspicion worse. It would have been quite impossible to keep any journey I made outside the Norbulingka a secret, unless a total curfew had been enforced throughout the town. The moment I prepared to go out, the word always went round and the whole of Lhasa turned up and lined the route to see me. And at that time, there were many extra people in the city who would also be certain to come. Most of the monks who had been at the Monlam Festival had left, but a few thousand still remained, and there were also several thousand refugees. At a rough estimate, there may have been a hundred thousand people in Lhasa just then, and perhaps that was the highest population the city had ever had.

So to keep order along the route on the following day, my officials decided to post the usual Tibetan guards as far as the Stone Bridge which led into the Chinese area, and they also made plans to ensure that the crowd would not overflow beyond the bridge. On the afternoon of March ninth, they told the Tibetan police on duty along the road to warn people that on the next day there would be special traffic restrictions and nobody would be allowed beyond the bridge.

They took this precaution in all good faith, because crossing the bridge was not normally forbidden, and they thought there might be tragic consequences if people innocently crossed it to see me pass and the Chinese soldiers tried to force them back. But the result was the reverse of what they intended. A rumor spread at once throughout the city that the Chinese had made a plan to kidnap me. During the evening and night of the ninth of March excitement and agitation grew, and by the morning most of the people of Lhasa had decided spontaneously to prevent my visit to the Chinese camp at any cost.

There was another fact which made people all the more certain that a trap had been laid to abduct me. A meeting of the Chinese National Assembly was due to be held in Peking in the following month, and the Chinese had been pressing me to go. Knowing the mood of the people, I had been trying to avoid accepting the invitation, and had not given the Chinese government any definite answer. But in spite of that, just over a week before, they had announced in Peking that

I was coming. That announcement without my consent had already made people in Lhasa very angry, and naturally they concluded that the strange new invitation was simply a ruse to fly me out against my will to China.

There was also an even more somber suspicion in the people's minds. It was widely known in Tibet that in four different places in the eastern provinces, high lamas had been invited to parties by the Chinese army commanders and had never been seen again: three had been killed, and one imprisoned. It seemed that this method of luring people away from anyone who might try to protect them was a Chinese custom.

The suspicion of the ordinary people of Lhasa also spread among the officials of my government, through yet another unusual act by the Chinese authorities. Normally, when the Chinese invited me to any social function, they also invited all the highest Tibetan officials. But on this occasion, until the evening of the ninth of March, no officials except my own personal staff had been invited. Late that night, two Chinese officers came to the Norbulingka with invitation cards, but only for the six members of my Cabinet; and verbally they made the unusual request that the Cabinet members should not bring more than one servant with them. By custom, my Senior Chamberlain always accompanied me wherever I went, as the Chinese knew very well, but neither he nor any other officials were included in the invitation.

In spite of their suspicion, my officials did not try to persuade me not to go; but my Cabinet decided to accompany me, instead of going separately, which was the normal practice, because they felt that if anything unpleasant happened, they would at least have the satisfaction of not having left me alone.

The following day was destined to be the most momentous Lhasa had ever seen. At noon I was supposed to take the unprecedented step of entering the Chinese camp without an escort. But when I woke up that morning, I had no idea of what the day was really going to bring. I had slept badly because I had been worrying about it. At five I got up, and went as usual to my prayer room. Everything was perfectly orderly, and perfectly peaceful and familiar. The butter lamps were burning before the altars, and the small golden and silver bowls had been replenished with sweet-smelling saffron water, like liquid gold, and the fragrance of incense permeated the air. I offered prayers and medi-tated, and then I went downstairs and out to the garden, where I always liked to walk in the early morning.

At first I was preoccupied with my worries, but I soon forgot them in the beauty of the spring morning. The sky was cloudless. The rays of the sun were just touching the peak of the mountain behind the distant monastery of Drepung, and beginning to shine on the palace and chapels which stood in my Jewel Park. Everything was fresh and gay with spring: the spears of the new green grass, the del-icate buds on the poplar and willow trees, the lotus leaves in the lake thrusting up to the surface and unfolding to the sun—all was green. And since I was born in the Wood Hog Year, and wood is green, astrologers would have said that green was my lucky color. Indeed, for that reason my per-sonal prayer flags were green, and they were flying from the roof of my house and beginning to stir in a gentle morn-ing breeze.

That was the last brief moment of peace of mind I was to know. It was broken by shouts, sudden and discordant, from beyond the wall of the park. I listened, but I could not distinguish the words. I hurried indoors, found some of my officials, and sent them to find out what was happening. They soon came back to tell me that the people of Lhasa seemed to be streaming out of the city and surrounding the Norbulingka, and that they were shouting that they had come to protect me, and to stop the Chinese taking me to the camp.

Soon all the palaces were astir with anxious people. Messengers kept coming to me with further news. The crowd was countless—some said there were 30,000 people. They were in a state of turbulent excitement, and the shouts were furious anger against the Chinese. Hour by hour the turmoil grew. I myself went to pray in a small chapel which had been built by the Seventh Dalai Lama and dedicated to Mahakala, the militant aspect of Chenresi, endowed with the power of protection against evil. Eight monks had already been there for several days, offering continuous prayer.

Two members of my Cabinet, Liushar and Shasur, drove up to the palace about nine o'clock in Chinese army jeeps with Chinese drivers, which was their usual practice. The people grew even more excited when they saw the Chinese drivers, but the ministers did not have much difficulty in getting through the crowd and into the palace.

But a little later, another minister, Samdup Phodrang, drove up in his own car escorted by a Chinese officer. Then for a moment the crowd got out of control. Samdup Phodrang had only recently been appointed to the Cabinet, and only a few people in Lhasa knew him by sight. He was wearing a Tibetan robe of yellow silk, and he would probably have been able to come in through the gates without any trouble if he had been alone, but the crowd thought the car was Chinese and jumped to the conclusion that the Chinese officer had come to take me away. Somebody threw a stone at him—the panic reaction spread, and the car was bombarded with stones. One of them hit Samdup Phodrang on the temple and knocked him unconscious. Even when he was lying unconscious, the people did not recognize him; but thinking they had mistakenly injured one of my officials, some of them picked him up and carried him to the hospital of the Indian Consulate.

A little later still, another member of the Cabinet, Surkhang, approached the palace in his jeep, but he could not drive up to the gate because by then the crowd had completely blocked the road. He got out of the jeep some distance away and walked through the crowd and entered the gate with the help of a Tibetan official who was stationed there.

These three ministers, having been in the crowd themselves, all realized that something must be done very quickly to avert a crisis—they thought the crowd might try to attack the Chinese headquarters. They waited some time for Ngabo, who was also a member of the Cabinet, but he did not come. Later we learned that he had gone to the Chinese camp, apparently in the belief that I would be there, and then thought it would be unsafe for him to come out again—as indeed it might have been, for the Chinese would have sent an escort with him and they would have been stoned like Samdup Phodrang's escort.

But finally they decided they could not wait any longer, and the three of them held a meeting together with Chikyab Khempo, the Chief Official Abbot, who also had ministerial rank. Then they came to see me. They told me the people had decided I must not be taken to the Chinese camp for fear that I would be abducted and taken away to China. The crowd had already elected a kind of committee of sixty or seventy leaders, and taken an oath that if the Chinese insisted I should go, they would barricade the palace and make it impossible for me to be taken out of it. And the Cabinet told me the crowd was so alarmed and resolute that it really would not be safe for me to go.

By the time the Cabinet members came to see me, I could hear what the people were shouting: "The Chinese must go; leave Tibet to the Tibetans"—all their slogans demanded an end of the Chinese occupation and of Chinese interference with the Dalai Lama's rule. Hearing the shouts, I could feel the tension of these people. I had been born one of them, and I understood what they were feeling and knew that in their present state of mind they were uncontrollable. And that knowledge was confirmed, later in the morning, when

I heard with great pain and sorrow that a monastic official called Phakpala Khenchung had been manhandled and finally stoned to death by the angry mob. This man had become notorious in Lhasa because of his close association with the Chinese occupation forces. Earlier that morning he had attended a daily congregation of monastic officials called the Trungcha Ceremony, and for some unknown reason, about eleven o'clock, he rode towards the Norbulingka on a bicycle, wearing a semi-Chinese dress, dark glasses and a motorcyclist's dust mask, and carrying a pistol unconcealed in his belt. Some of the crowd took him for a Chinese in disguise; others thought he was bringing a message from the Chinese headquarters. Their anger and resentment against everything Chinese suddenly burst into fury, and murder was the tragic result.

This outbreak of violence gave me great distress. I told my Cabinet to tell the Chinese general that I could not attend the performance, and also that it would be unwise for anyone from his headquarters to come to the Norbulingka at present, because that might anger the crowd still further. My Senior Chamberlain telephoned to the general's interpreter and gave him this message, with my apologies and regret. The interpreter agreed that my decision was correct, and said he would give the message to the general.

At the same time I also told the Cabinet to tell the people who had surrounded the palace that if they did not wish me to go to the Chinese camp, I would not go. Minister Surkhang got in touch with the leaders whom the people had chosen and told them I had canceled my visit, and about noon a loudspeaker was used to make a similar announcement to the crowd. It was greeted with jubilant cheers from outside the gates.

The mental stress of that morning was something I had not experienced before during the brief period of my leadership of the people of Tibet. I felt as if I were standing between two volcanoes, each likely to erupt at any moment.

On one side, there was the vehement, unequivocal, unanimous protest of my people against the Chinese regime; on the other, there was the armed might of a powerful and aggressive occupation force. If there was a clash between the two, the result was a foregone conclusion. The Lhasan people would be ruthlessly massacred in thousands, and Lhasa and the rest of Tibet would see a fullscale military rule with all its persecution and tyranny. The immediate cause of the explosive situation was the question whether I should go to the Chinese camp or not. But at the same time, I was the only possible peacemaker, and I knew that at all costs, for the sake of my own people, I must try to calm the anger of the people and pacify the Chinese who would certainly be even angrier.

I had hoped that the announcement that I was not going would end the demonstration, and that the people would go home in peace. But it was not enough. Their leaders said they would not go unless I assured them I had not only canceled the visit for that day, but had also decided not to accept any invitation in the future to go to the Chinese camp. Nothing seemed too high a price to pay to avert a disaster, so I gave the assurance they wanted. Then most of these chosen leaders left; but most of the rest of the people still stayed outside the palace and would not go away.

At about one o'clock I told my three ministers to go to see General Tan Kuan-sen and explain the whole situation to him personally. There was still a vast multitude outside the gates determined to prevent anyone leaving, and the appearance of the ministers at the gates made the people suspect that I might be following them. The ministers explained to the crowd, with some difficulty, that I had instructed them to go to the Chinese headquarters and tell the general that I could not come to his theatrical performance. On this assurance the crowd insisted on searching the ministers' cars to make sure that I had not been hidden in one of them, but when they had satisfied themselves about that, they let the

ministers go. During that discussion at the gate, the spokes-
men of the crowd said they had decided to choose a bodyguard from amongst themselves and post it all around the
palace to prevent the Chinese getting in to take me away.
The ministers tried to persuade them not to do that, but they
would not accept their advice.

When the ministers came back that afternoon, they told
me what had happened at the Chinese headquarters. General Tan Kuan-sen was not there when they arrived, but ten
other officers were waiting for them, apparently engaged in
a serious conversation; and with them was Ngabo, my other
Cabinet minister, dressed in Tibetan clothes instead of the
Chinese general's uniform which he had recently had to wear
when he was in attendance at the Chinese offices. Ngabo
was sitting with the officers, but he did not seem to be taking part in their discussion. He did not leave his seat to join
the ministers when they entered.

For some time, not a word was spoken by either side
about the events of the day. The Chinese officers seemed
to be unconcerned, and they inquired politely about the ministers' health. But the atmosphere suddenly changed when
General Tan Kuan-sen came in and took charge of the proceedings.

The ministers told me the general seemed very angry when
he came into the room. His appearance was intimidating,
and the ministers rose nervously from their seats to show
him respect. For a few minutes, he seemed to be speechless
with rage, and he did not greet the ministers. Surkhang
opened the conversation by telling him that I had sent them
to explain what had happened to prevent me from attending
the dramatic performance. He said I had had every intention of coming, but the people's wishes were so strongly
against it that I had had to give up the idea. The other two
ministers also added their explanations. By the time the interpreter had finished, the general was visibly red in the face.
He rose from his seat and started pacing up and down the

room, apparently beside himself with anger. After a great appearance of effort, he managed to control himself and sat down again. Then with studied deliberation and slowness of speech, he began a harangue against the ministers and "Tibetan reactionaries." Although he seemed to be trying to control his temper, his voice often rose sharply and his simmering anger burst out in rude and abusive language. He was using Chinese words which are never spoken in any polite Chinese society. The general point of the harangue was that the government of Tibet had been secretly organizing agitation by the people against the Chinese authorities and helping the Khampas in their rebellion. Tibetan officials had defied the orders of the Chinese and refused to disarm the Khampas in Lhasa—and now, drastic measures would be taken to crush the opposition to Chinese rule.

Two other generals made similar tirades. One of them declared the time had come to "destroy all these reactionaries. . . . Our government has been tolerant so far," he said, "but this is rebellion. This is the breaking point. We shall act now, so be prepared!"

My bewildered ministers took these harangues as an ultimatum of military action if the popular agitation did not cease at once. They were convinced the prospect was dangerous and involved the safety of the person of the Dalai Lama; and they felt that if anything happened to me, there would be nothing left of Tibet. They tried to counsel patience. Shasur told the general that the Chinese should try to understand the ordinary Tibetan people and be patient and tolerant. They should not make a serious situation worse by retaliation. And he assured him that the Cabinet would do all that was possible to prevent an outbreak of lawlessness among the Khampas or any other Tibetans who might be foolhardy enough to try to provoke a clash of arms with the Chinese occupation forces. But the Chinese generals would not accept this assurance or listen to this advice.

Deeply perturbed, the ministers came back to the Norbulingka about five in the evening. By then a part of the crowd had dispersed, though there was still a large number of people surrounding the main gate. Those who had left, we learned later, had gone into the city to hold public meetings and stage mass demonstrations against the Chinese. At the meetings they denounced the Seventeen-Point Agreement on the ground that the Chinese had broken it, and they demanded once more that the Chinese should withdraw. At six the same evening, about seventy members of the government, mostly junior officials, together with the leaders chosen by the crowd and members of the Kusung Regiment (the Dalai Lama's bodyguard) held a meeting inside the Norbulingka grounds and endorsed the declaration which had been made at the meetings in the city. They also made a declaration that Tibet no longer recognized Chinese authority; and soon afterwards, the Kusung Regiment declared that they would no longer take orders from Chinese officers, and they discarded the Chinese uniforms which they had been made to wear and appeared again in their Tibetan dress.

As soon as I heard of these decisions, I sent instructions to the leaders stating that their duty was to reduce the existing tension and not aggravate it—to be patient and meet all events with calm and forbearance. But by then the resentment of the people was so bitter, and their suspicion of the Chinese so great, that my advice seemed to have no effect on them at all.

Late in the evening of the same day, a letter from General Tan Kuan-sen was delivered to me. It was the first of three letters he sent me within the next few days, and I replied to all of them.

These letters were published by the Chinese, after all the events in Lhasa were over, to support their own propaganda. They used them to try to prove that I wanted to seek shelter in the Chinese headquarters, but was kept under duress in the Norbulingka by what they called a "reactionary clique," and finally abducted out of the country to India against my will. This story was repeated in some of the foreign press which was favorably inclined towards Communist China, and I was shocked to hear over a year later that it had been quoted by a member of the British peerage in the House of Lords. As it is the very opposite of the truth, I want to describe the circumstances in which these letters were written, and my reasons for writing them, and to say once and for all that when I left Lhasa I went of my own free will. The decision was mine alone, made under the stress of a desperate situation. I was not abducted by my entourage; I was not under any pressure to go from anybody, except in so far as every Tibetan in Lhasa could see by then that the Chinese were preparing to shell my palace and that my life would be in danger if I stayed there.

The general's letters to me were written in friendly terms which would have seemed more sincere if I had not already been told of his rage by my ministers. He said he was concerned for my safety and invited me to take refuge in his camp.

I replied to all his letters to gain time—time for anger to cool on both sides, and time for me to urge moderation of the Lhasan people. And to this end I thought it would be foolish to argue with the general, or to point out that Chinese protection from my own people was the very last thing I needed. On the contrary, I decided to reply in a way which I hoped would calm him down. And this I could only do by seeming to accept his sympathy and welcome his advice. In my first letter I told him how embarrassed I had been at my people's action in preventing me from coming to his entertainment. In the second letter, I told him I had given orders that the people surrounding the Norbulingka should disperse, and I concurred with his point of view that these people, under the pretext of protecting me, were only working to undermine the relations between the Chinese and our government. And in the third letter, I also added that I must separate the people who supported new ideas and those who opposed them before I could visit his headquarters.

Even if I had thought at the time that these letters would be quoted against me later, I would still have written them, because my most urgent moral duty at that moment was to prevent a totally disastrous clash between my unarmed people and the Chinese army.

And perhaps I may repeat once more that I could not approve of violence, and so I could not approve of the violent attitude the people of Lhasa were showing. I could and do appreciate the affection for me, as the symbol of Tibet, an attitude which was the immediate cause of the anger they were showing against the Chinese on that fateful day. I could not blame them for their anxiety for my safety, because the Dalai Lama represented most of what they lived and worked for. But I was certain that what they were doing could only lead to disaster if they continued, and as Head of State I had to try by every means to curb their feelings and stop them bringing about their own destruction under the weight of the Chinese army. So the advice I gave them was given in the fullest sincerity, and although my letters to the Chinese general were written to disguise my true intentions, I felt and still feel that they were justified.

But by the following day, the eleventh of March, it was clear that the Lhasan people were becoming even more difficult to control. On that day they posted six guards near the Cabinet office inside the Norbulingka and warned the ministers that they would not be allowed to leave. Presumably they suspected that the Cabinet might make some kind of compromise with the Chinese and so defeat the popular demand that the Chinese should leave Tibet. The Cabinet convened an emergency meeting. Only four of the six ministers were present, because Samdup Phodrang was still too ill from his injury to be able to come, and Ngabo refused to come out of the Chinese camp. But these four decided to make another effort to persuade the people to call off their demonstration, and they sent for the leaders of the crowd.

At that meeting, the leaders seemed to be more amenable and they told the Cabinet they would tell the people to disperse. They also said they were sorry Samdup Phodrang had been hurt, and asked the Cabinet to deliver some presents from them to him by way of apology.

In that somewhat more conciliatory mood, the people probably would have dispersed before long, and the efforts which I and the Cabinet had been making to bring the demonstration to a peaceful end would probably have succeeded; but then two more letters arrived from the general, one to me and one to the Cabinet. The letter to the Cabinet completely defeated our efforts. It said that the "rebels" had put up barricades on the north side of Lhasa, on the road towards China, and told the Cabinet to order them to be removed at once. It warned the Cabinet that if this was not done, "serious consequences would follow, for which the responsibility would rest with Surkhang, Liushar, Shasur, and Donyerchemo."

The Cabinet sent for the leaders of the people again and advised them to remove the barricades, so that the Chinese could not find an excuse in them for more repression. But that advice had exactly the wrong effect. The leaders absolutely refused to demolish the barricades. They said they had put them there to protect the Norbulingka by keeping Chinese reinforcements out of the city, and if the Chinese wanted them removed, the obvious conclusion was that they did mean to attack the Palace and capture the Dalai Lama. They also said that the Chinese themselves had put up barricades in front of the temple and taken similar precautions to protect their Tibetan supporters, such as Ngabo. If the Chinese could use barricades to protect Ngabo, they asked, why should they object to the people of Lhasa protecting the Palace? This was unfortunate logic, but the leaders could not be persuaded to see the Chinese orders in any other way;

and the unhappy result was that they became more apprehensive about my safety and refused to disperse the crowd. The people became more uncompromising, appointed six commanders from among themselves to strengthen the defense of the Palace, and announced that they would not leave the Palace unguarded whatever happened.

This development distressed me very much. I felt it was one step more toward disaster. So I decided to speak to the people's leaders myself. I sent for them, and all seventy of them came, and in the presence of the Cabinet and other senior officials I did my best to dissuade them from their actions. I told them the Chinese general had not compelled me to accept his invitation; I had been consulted and given my consent before the invitation was issued. I said I was not in any fear of personal danger from the Chinese, and they must not create a situation which could have such serious consequences for the people. I knew this would offend their feelings, but I had to tell them what I felt in the sincerest hope that the normal peace of Lhasa might be restored to some extent.

The leaders did not question my advice or contradict me. They quietly left the meeting and held a conference among themselves by the outer gate of the Palace. They agreed that it was impossible for them to disobey my orders, but there was a long argument about what would happen to me if their protection was withdrawn. In the end, they carried out my wishes to the extent of holding no more meetings within the Norbulingka. Instead of that, they met at the village of Shol, at the foot of the Potala, and sent reports of their decisions to me and the Cabinet after each meeting. These reports amounted to a repetition of their earlier declarations: they would continue to protect me, and the Chinese must leave Lhasa and Tibet and allow the Tibetans to manage their own affairs.

So the next two days dragged by. The situation seemed to be static and the problems to be insoluble, but obviously things could not go on as they were. Something must happen soon, for better or worse.

General Tan Kuan-sen's third and last letter to me arrived on the morning of the sixteenth of March, and I replied to it on the same day. Afterwards, the Chinese published both these letters. But they did not say that in the same envelope with the general's letter there was another sent to me by Ngabo. He had not attended any Cabinet meetings since the crisis started. Now he wrote to warn me that he did not think there was much chance of peace. He suggested that I should try to "destroy the hostile designs of the reactionaries," and cut all my connections with the people's leaders. He said he gathered the people had an "evil plan" to remove me from the Norbulingka. If that was true, it would be very dangerous for me, because the Chinese had taken the strictest measures to prevent my escape. And even if I did escape, he said, in the present international situation I would never be able to return to Lhasa. And then he said: "If Your Holiness with a few trusted officers of the bodyguard can stay within the inner wall, and hold a position there, and inform General Tan Kuan-sen exactly which building you will occupy, they certainly intend that this building will not be damaged."

So Ngabo knew what we had only guessed: that the Chinese did intend to destroy the palace and the crowd, but still wanted to do it, if they could, without also killing me.

He wrote to the Cabinet too, more or less repeating what he had written to me, and urging them to get the people away from the Palace, or at least to see that they stayed outside the walls. He said he understood the difficulties, and if they could not make the people go, they should try to take me out of the Palace and into the Chinese camp for my own safety. Meanwhile, they should send a sketch map of the Palace showing the position of the building I was occupying.

I replied to the general's letter in much the same way that I had written to him before. It still seemed to me that the only chance of persuading him not to attack the crowd and the Palace was to seem to fall in with his wishes. I did not tell him which building I was in. I felt that so long as the Chinese did not know exactly where I was, there was still some chance they would not use artillery; if we told them, it seemed certain that the rest of the Norbulingka would be laid in ruins. I told him again that I would come to his camp as soon as possible. I had no intention of going, but I hoped this promise would persuade him to delay his order to attack and enable us to get the people away in time. That was the last of the letters I wrote to him.

The whole atmosphere round the Palace by then was extremely tense. Outside its inner wall was a vast multitude of excited angry people. Most of them had armed themselves with sticks, spades or knives, or whatever other weapons they could muster. Among them were some soldiers and Khampas with rifles, a few machine guns, and even fourteen or fifteen mortars. Hand to hand, with fists or swords, one Tibetan would have been worth a dozen Chinese—recent experiences in the eastern provinces had confirmed this old belief. But it was obvious that their strength was useless against the heavy equipment which the Chinese could bring to wipe them out. Practically, they had nothing to fight with except their own determination to protect me.

But within the inner wall, in the immediate precincts of the Palace, everything had the appearance of calm and peace. There were no signs of anything untoward. The garden was quiet as usual. The peacocks strutted about with their plumes held high, unconcerned about the human turmoil; singing birds were flying from tree to tree, mixing their music with that of the fountains near the rock garden; the tame deer, the fish, and the brahmini ducks and white cranes were as placid as ever. A contingent of my bodyguard, out of uniform, was even watering the lawns and flower beds. The atmosphere was still typical of Tibet, where for centuries people have sought for peace of mind and devoted themselves through their religion to finding the path towards freedom from sorrow and suffering.

On the sixteenth of March news began to come in of the Chinese preparations for destroying this peaceful place. People reported to the Cabinet, and thence to me, that all the artillery in the district was being brought in to sites within range of the city, and of the Norbulingka in particular. A man who worked on a hydroelectric plant which was being built about eight miles east of Lhasa reported that four mountain guns and twenty-eight heavy machine guns, which were usually kept there, had been secretly taken to Lhasa during the night of the fourteenth, escorted by several truck loads of Chinese soldiers. A district official from Bomtue, fifteen miles east of Lhasa, told us of twenty heavy guns which had been sent toward the city. On the evening of the thirteenth, and again on the fifteenth, two giant Chinese military vehicles with three soldiers in each were found near the northern gate of the Palace with mechanical instruments, apparently taking measurements. When they saw that the people were watching them they hurriedly drove away, and the people's guards who saw them jumped to the conclusion that they were taking the measurements for ranging heavy guns on the Palace. In the night a hundred new Chinese trucks were seen moving slowly toward the Potala, and from there to the Chinese camp. On the following morning, fifteen or twenty Chinese in civilian clothes were seen perched on telegraph poles, apparently mending the wires, but the people concluded they were taking more readings for range finding. Our people did not know much about artillery and they may have been wrong, but that was what they believed.

Besides all these observations, there were rumors of fresh troops arriving from China by air. By the night of the sixteenth, the people were certain that the Chinese were about to shell the Palace, and that danger might come without warning at any moment. Their feelings rose to a state of panic, but they still would not leave the Palace and abandon it and me. Everyone in authority tried to pacify them, but their fury against the Chinese was uncontrollable. For the crowd and for my ministers and myself, that was a very disturbed night, and nobody could sleep.

When morning came, rumors were still springing up and spreading, and destruction still seemed imminent. It seemed to me and my Cabinet that the situation was completely desperate. We held a meeting. There was only one question to discuss: how could we prevent the destruction of the Palace and the massacre of the thousands of people round it? We could only decide to make another appeal to the Chinese general not to use force to disperse the crowd, but to wait till the Cabinet had tried again to persuade them to leave in peace. So the Cabinet hurriedly wrote a letter to Ngabo to this effect. They said the people were acting foolishly and under the stress of emotion, but there was still hope that they could be persuaded to leave the Palace in the end. And they also suggested that Ngabo should help them to take me to the Chinese camp. They pointed out that this would be very difficult, because the whole area round the Palace was controlled by the people, but they said they would do their best. They sent a special code with that letter and asked Ngabo to use it in his reply, because the popular guards round the Palace had started to censor any letters which came into their hands. The sole purpose of that letter, of course, was to conciliate the Chinese general. In fact, it would have been quite impossible for me to have gone to the Chinese camp. I would indeed have been willing to go there and throw myself on the mercy of the Chinese if that would have prevented the massacre of my people; but the people would never have let me do it.

It was very difficult to send that letter, because the popular guards were on the alert and would not allow officials to leave the Palace. But one of Minister Shasur's attendants succeeded in slipping out, pretending he was going shopping in the city, and he managed to deliver the letter to

Ngabo and come back with his reply. This was a brief polite acknowledgment. He said he was pleased at the Cabinet's proposal that I should be moved to the Chinese camp and promised to send a detailed answer later; but that answer did not come until after all was over.

About four o'clock that afternoon, while I was discussing Ngabo's answer with the ministers, we heard the boom of two heavy mortar shells fired from a nearby Chinese camp. And we also heard the splash of the shells in a marsh outside the northern gate.

At those two isolated shots, consternation and anger reached a final climax in the crowd. No explanation has ever been given of why they were fired, but those who heard them could only think the attack had begun and the Palace was the target. Within the Palace everyone felt the end had come and that something drastic had to be done without any more delay, but nobody could decide what to do.

It was I who had to find the answer and make the decision; but with my inexperience in the affairs of the world it was not easy. I have no fear of death. I was not afraid of being one of the victims of the Chinese attack. I honestly believe that my strict religious training has given me enough strength to face the prospect of leaving my present body without any apprehension. I felt then, as I always feel, that I am only a mortal being and an instrument of the never dying spirit of my Master, and that the end of one mortal frame is not of any great consequence. But I knew my people and the officials of my government could not share my feelings. To them the person of the Dalai Lama was supremely precious. They believed the Dalai Lama represented Tibet and the Tibetan way of life, something dearer to them than anything else. They were convinced that if my body perished at the hands of the Chinese, the life of Tibet would also come to an end.

So when the Chinese guns sounded that warning of death, the first thought in the mind of every official within the

Palace, and every humble member of the vast concourse around it, was that my life must be saved and I must leave the Palace and leave the city at once. The decision was not a small matter; the stakes were high; the whole future of Tibet depended on it. There was no certainty that escape was physically possible at all—Ngabo had assured us it was not. If I did escape from Lhasa, where was I to go, and how could I reach asylum? Above all, would the Chinese destroy our holy city and massacre our people if I went—or would the people scatter from the Palace when they heard that I had gone, and so perhaps would some lives be saved? Our minds were overwhelmed by such unanswerable questions. Everything was uncertain, except the compelling anxiety of all my people to get me away before the orgy of Chinese destruction and massacre began. This was the only positive worldly guide I had in making my decision. If I decided to stay, I would add even more to the distress of my people and of my closest friends. I decided to go. I need hardly say I prayed for guidance and received it.

We could not tell where the journey would lead or how it would end, but all the people closest to me wanted to come with me: the four members of my Cabinet who were present, my tutors, my personal officials, my bodyguard, and, of course, the closest members of my family. My mother had come into the Norbulingka when the trouble started and had brought my youngest brother with her—the brother who had been reborn after he had died when he was two. My elder sister, who was married to Kusung Depon, the commander of my bodyguard, was also there. Two of my brothers were in America, and the other was in India—so was my younger sister who attended school in Darjeeling.

So it was to be a large party, and we would need the help of an even larger number of people. Yet we had to keep it secret, not only from the Chinese, but also from the mass of the crowd outside. Everyone suspected there might be Chinese spies among the crowd. Besides, if the crowd had known I was going, thousands of them would have followed me to offer me their protection, and the Chinese would certainly have seen them, and the massacre would have begun at once.

I and my ministers consulted the popular leaders, and they instantly saw that this had to be done without telling the mass of the people who had elected them. They gave us the best of cooperation. I wrote a letter to them too, and left it in the Norbulingka with instructions that it should be delivered to them the next day. In it I begged them again not to open fire unless they were attacked, and promised them more detailed orders as soon as I was away from the immediate dangers and restrictions of my present situation.

There was no time to take anything which was not essential with us; we had to be well away from Lhasa before the dawn. The ministers had my Seal of Office, the Seal of the Cabinet, and a few papers which happened to be in the Norbulingka. Most of the state papers were in the Cabinet office or the Potala, and they had to be abandoned. So did all our personal belongings. All I could take was one or two changes of Lama robes. We could not go to the Treasury for any funds, or to the Potala for any of the immeasurable wealth of jewels and treasures which I had inherited.

We decided to leave in small parties. The first essential was to cross the river. The Norbulingka and the Chinese camp were both close to its northern bank, and it was only on the southern side that we had any chance of getting away.

The steward of one of the monasteries was with us and he was sent out to cross the river and arrange for horses and an escort on the other side. Doji Dadul, the commander of the second battalion of the Tibetan army, went out with about a hundred soldiers to guard a point southeast of the Norbulingka, where the river is narrow and comparatively easy to cross. And at that early stage the whole plan nearly ended in disaster. These men had only gone half a mile when they suddenly sighted a Chinese patrol, apparently making for the same spot. They set up their Bren gun at once and fired five shots. That was quick thinking and it saved the situation. The Chinese knew there were armed Khampas near the river, and in the dark they could not see the size or the nature of the Tibetan party; so they retreated to the safety of their camp, which was only a short distance away.

When everything was ready, I went to the chapel of Mahakala. I had always gone to that chapel to say good-by when I went on long journeys. Monks were still there, offering their constant prayers, and they did not know what was about to happen; but I offered a scarf at the altar as a symbol of farewell. I knew they would wonder why I did so, but I also knew they would never express their surprise.

As I came out of the chapel I met my Senior Chamberlain and the Chief Official Abbot and Kusung Depon. The Chamberlain and the Abbot were already dressed in ordinary laymen's clothes. They had been wearing them whenever they went out for several days, but I had never seen them dressed like that before. We had agreed to meet at the gate in the inner wall at ten. We synchronized our watches. Then I went to several other chapels and blessed them, and then to my own rooms; and I waited there alone.

While I waited for the time to come, I knew that my mother and my sister and my small brother would be leaving: we had agreed that they should be the first to go. It was easier for them than for the rest of us to leave the Palace, because they had been living outside its inner yellow wall. My mother and sister were to be dressed as Khampa men. I was to go next, and the Cabinet ministers, my tutors, and a few others were to make the third and final party.

A soldier's clothes and a fur cap had been left for me, and about half past nine I took off my monk's habit and put them on. And then, in that unfamiliar dress, I went to my prayer room for the last time. I sat down on my usual throne and opened the book of Lord Buddha's teachings which lay before it, and I read to myself till I came to a passage in which Lord Buddha told a disciple to be of good courage. Then I closed the book and blessed the room, and turned down the lights. As I went out, my mind was drained of all emotion. I was aware of my own sharp footfalls on the floor of beaten earth, and the ticking of the clock in the silence.

At the inner door of my house there was a single soldier waiting for me, and another at the outer door. I took a rifle from one of them and slung it on my shoulder to complete my disguise. The soldiers followed me, and I walked down through the dark garden which contained so many of the happiest memories of my life.

At the garden gates and the gate of the inner wall, Kusung Depon had told the guards to disperse. He met me at the first gate, and my other two companions at the second. As we passed the holy library near the Mahakala Temple, we bared our heads in homage and farewell. We crossed the park together, towards the gate in the outer wall, the Abbot and the Chamberlain and the Commander of the Bodyguard in front, and myself and the other two soldiers behind them. I took off my glasses, thinking that people would hardly know my face without them.

The gate was shut. My Chamberlain went on ahead and told the guards he was going on a tour of inspection. They saluted him, and opened the massive lock.

Only once before in my life, when I was taken to Yatung nine years before, had I been out of the gate of the Norbulingka without a ceremonial procession. When we reached it, I saw dimly in the darkness the groups of my people who were still watching it, but none of them noticed the humble soldier, and I walked out unchallenged towards the dark road beyond.

▣ 11 ▣

ESCAPE

On our way down to the river, we passed a large crowd of people, and my Chamberlain stopped to talk to their leaders. A few of them had been warned I was leaving that night, but of course the crowd in general did not know. While they talked, I stood and waited, trying to look like a soldier. It was not pitch dark, but I could not see well without my glasses, and I could not tell whether people were looking at me with curiosity or not. I was glad when the conversation ended.

We came to the river bank above the crossing place and had to walk down it, on white sandbanks interspersed with dark clumps of bushes. The Abbot is a big man, and he had chosen to carry an enormous sword, and I am sure he was ready to do destruction with it—at least, he adopted a very threatening attitude at every bush. But none of them concealed an enemy.

We crossed in coracles. On the other bank we met my family. My ministers and tutors, who had come out of the

Norbulingka hidden under a tarpaulin in a truck, also caught up with us there. About thirty Khampa soldiers were waiting for us, with three of their leaders: Kunga Samten, Tempa Thargye, and a very brave boy of only twenty called Wangchug Tsering. A boy called Losang Yishi was also there. He was one of the boys who had been taken to the school in Peking but had resisted Chinese indoctrination for the whole of the five years he was there. He died fighting two days later.

We exchanged scarves with these leaders. They had arranged everything as well as anyone could in the circumstances. The steward of the monastery had collected ponies for us all, although he had not been able to get any good saddles. After hurried greetings in low voices, we mounted and rode off without delay. The first few miles were likely to be the most dangerous.

There was no road over there, only a narrow stony track which skirted across a hill above the river. To the right we could see the lights of the Chinese camp. We were easily in range, and there was no telling what patrols they had posted along the dark banks of the river below us. Even closer we passed an island where the Chinese constantly drove in trucks to collect stone from a quarry—even at night. If one of them came we would be caught in the headlights. The track was hardly visible as we rode along it. The clink of the horseshoes on the stones seemed very loud. We thought patrols might hear it, but we had to hurry. I lost the track once, and had to turn my pony and go back. Then we saw flickering torches behind us, and it seemed for a while that the Chinese were close on our trail. But it was Tibetan soldiers, trying to guide some others of our party who had taken the wrong track and lost their way completely.

But we all passed that danger spot successfully and met again on the river bank about three miles downstream. Below that point, the river was so shallow that trucks could be driven across it, and if the Chinese had been alerted they might have driven down the other bank and cut us off there. So one of the officers and a few soldiers were left there as a rearguard. The rest of us rode onward steadily, away from the city, into the quiet empty countryside.

For a long way we saw no sign of life at all. But about three in the morning a dog barked, and we saw a house ahead. I sent my Chamberlain forward to find out where we were, and who the owner of the house was. He discovered that the name of the place was Namgyalgang. The owner was a simple kind man, and two of our escort had already been there to warn him to expect a very important guest. I was tired by then, and I rested there a little while. It was the first of many humble Tibetan houses whose owners sheltered me, without any thought of the risk, some knowing, and some not knowing, who I was.

There Wangchug Tsering, the admirable twenty-year-old Khampa leader, left us to take 400 of his men to guard us against attack from beyond the river. He had already detailed two or three hundred other Khampas to defend our route.

When I left the Norbulingka, and throughout this first hectic part of the journey, I was not thinking of going straight to India. I still hoped to be able to stay somewhere in Tibet. It was out of the question, in any case, to take either of the usual routes to India, which led southwest from Lhasa, because they were, of course, heavily guarded by Chinese. Instead, we were heading south and southeast from Lhasa. In that direction, there is a vast area of roadless mountains which the Chinese army would have found very difficult to penetrate in any strength. And that almost impregnable area was one of the principal strongholds of the Khampas and the other Tibetans who had joined them as guerrilla fighters. And from the heart of those mountains, across the main range of the Himalayas, several tracks led over the frontier and down to the state of Bhutan and so to India. They had been used for centuries by Tibetan and Bhutanese traders, so that if the worst came to the worst we would always have a line of retreat behind us.

But before we could reach this possible sanctuary in the mountains, we had to cross the wide Brahmaputra River, which is called the Tsang Po in Tibet, and before we could reach the river, we had one high mountain pass to cross: the Che-la. There was a danger that if the Chinese discovered I had gone they would put out patrols along the Tsang Po, so we had to push on, to cross it as quickly as possible.

We reached the foot of the Che-la about eight in the morning, and stopped there to have some tea. The sun was just rising above the peaks and gilding the plain behind us, but we were still in the shadow of the mountains when we began the long steep climb towards the pass. The way was rough and weary, and it took us well above the snow line. Some of the ponies and mules began to lag behind. But our spirits were raised by an old man called Tashi Norbu who joined us while we were climbing and offered me a graceful pure white horse. I accepted it gratefully, and all my party were happier, because Tibetans look on such a gift as a very propitious sign.

Che-la means Sandy Pass, and beyond the summit we found steep slopes of sand which we could run down, leaving our ponies to follow the winding track—but still it took us three or four hours to cross the pass. When at last we came down to the level ground in the valley of the Tsang Po, a heavy dust storm broke out suddenly and almost blinded us, but it was a comfort to think that if the Chinese were patrolling the valley, it would blind them too.

We found no human habitations near the foot of the pass, but we knew that about ten miles to the east—downstream—there was a ferry. It was the only way to cross, so we had to take the chance that the Chinese might have reached it first. But all went well. On the far bank of the river by the ferry, there is a little village called Kyeshong, which means Happy Valley. As the ferry boat approached the other shore, we could see a large crowd which had gathered to receive us, and when we approached we could distinguish Khampa soldiers among them, and village yeomen with white and yellow badges on their arms—men of the Volunteer Army who had joined the Khampas. When we landed, we found them deeply distressed by what they had heard of the events in Lhasa. And when we rode on I saw many of them weeping. Kyeshong was the first village we had passed through on our journey, and perhaps that fact, and perhaps its name, made me even sadder as we rode away. There, I thought, were the people of Tibet who had lived in their Happy Valley for centuries in perfect peace and harmony, and now grim fear stood over them and threatened all they lived for. Yet their morale was high and their courage was indomitable. I knew that whether I asked for their help or not, they would protect me with their lives.

With the river and these stalwart people behind us, we were safe for the moment from pursuit. We rode on to a monastery called Ra-me, where we had decided to rest for the night. We reached it about half past four that afternoon. We had been riding fast for nearly eighteen hours with only the briefest halts, and neither we nor our ponies could have gone much farther. While we rested, we worried more and more about those of the party who were still behind us, but by nine o'clock in the evening the last of them had come in.

My ministers wrote two letters that evening, one to Ngabo and the other to Samdup Phodrang, the two ministers who had been left behind in Lhasa, urging them to do their best to help Tibet, and saying they had no doubt that all of them shared the same hopes about the freedom of our country.

By then our party had increased to 100, and we were escorted by about 350 Tibetan soldiers, and at least fifty guerrillas. From Ra-me, a detachment of about 100 men was sent to the southwest, to protect us in case the Chinese approached from the direction of the main road into India. The rest of us rode on for the next five days into the heart of the mountains by the narrow stony tracks which are typical of old Tibet. By day we divided into several groups; each night we stopped in a village or a monastery. Sometimes we had no guerrilla leaders with us. They came and went, keeping in touch with all the isolated bands who were living in the mountains, and we knew that we were surrounded by faithful determined men whom we never saw. Not all of them knew whom they were defending. The first night after lodging at Ra-me, we stayed in a big village called Dophu Choekhor, where guerrillas are still keeping up a desperate fight against the Chinese invaders to this day. The whole village came out to welcome us, but most of them did not recognize me in the unfamiliar clothes I was wearing, nor did most of the monks in the neighboring monastery.

During this five day march, our plans were crystallizing, and we made up our minds to halt for a day at a place called Chenye, in order to give ourselves time for a thorough discussion about the future, and to send out instructions to officials in Lhasa, to the Khampas, and other guerrillas. Our plan was that we should go on until we reached a place called Lhuntse Dzong. This is not very far from the border. It had one of the biggest forts in the area, and it had good communications with the rest of southern Tibet. There, we thought, I should stay, and try to reopen peaceful negotiations with the Chinese. We hoped that while I remained in Tibet the Chinese might see some advantage in coming to terms and might still be prevented from shelling Lhasa.

We reached Chenye in safety. A day or two before, I had taken my young brother into my party, thinking that my mother and sister would be able to travel faster without him. And so they did. They were soon a whole stage ahead of the rest of us, with a small escort of Khampas, and we did not see them again until a much later stage of our journey. It was one weight off my mind to know that they were comparatively safe. We had brought a battery radio receiver with us, and we had been listening to all the news bulletins we could pick up, in the hope of hearing news about Lhasa; and I think it was at Chenye that we first heard Lhasa mentioned. It was the Voice of America, but it only reported unrest in the city and added that my whereabouts was unknown.

We stayed for the night in a small monastery at Chenye, but everyone advised us to go on one more stage—to another monastery called Chongay Riudechen—before we made our halt, because that was a bigger place and we would find it easier from there to get in touch with all the guerrilla leaders. So we set off on another eight-hour ride. But before we ended it, our plans were in the melting pot again, for direct news of what was happening in Lhasa began to catch up with us.

Soon after we left Chenye we saw a group of horsemen coming towards us, and as they approached us we recognized among them Tsepon Namseling, one of the officials who had been sent by the Cabinet seven months before to persuade the Khampas to give up armed resistance, and who had joined the Khampas and never come back to Lhasa. We stopped, and I had a long talk with him. He gave me detailed news of the disposition of the Chinese troops and of all the skirmishes the Khampas had already had with them. But the devastating news he brought was that Lhasa had already been bombarded.

He had only heard this indirectly, but soon afterwards a letter from my private secretary, Khenchung Tara, was brought to me. I had last seen him in Lhasa, but the letter was written from the Ra-me Monastery. He had not left Lhasa until after the shelling had started, and he was wounded: he had been hit by a shell splinter while he was still inside the Norbulingka. And from him, and from other eye witnesses in the next few days, we were able to reconstruct the whole story of the disaster I had striven so hard to prevent.

The shelling had begun at two o'clock in the morning of

March twentieth, just over forty-eight hours after I left, and before the Chinese had discovered that I had gone. All that day they shelled the Norbulingka, and then they turned their artillery on the city, the Potala, the temple, and the neighboring monasteries. Nobody knows how many of the people of Lhasa were killed, but thousands of bodies could be seen inside and outside the Norbulingka. Some of the main buildings within the Norbulingka were practically destroyed, and all of the others were damaged in different degrees, except the chapel of Mahakala which had a miraculous escape. Within the city, houses were demolished or set on fire, the golden roofs of the main temple were holed, and many of the chapels around it were ruined. In the Potala, the western wing was seriously damaged, part of the rooms I had used there were destroyed, and so were the government school, the main gate, the army headquarters, and other houses in the village of Shol. One of the shells fell in the room which housed the golden mausoleum of the Thirteenth Dalai Lama. Chakpori, one of the Tibetan medical colleges, was almost razed to the ground. In the great monastery of Sera there was the same useless wanton devastation.

By the end of the first day, when the Norbulingka was a deserted smoking ruin full of dead, the Chinese entered it. The few Tibetans who, like Ngabo, were in the Chinese camp had been desperately anxious about my fate. That evening, the Chinese were seen to be going from corpse to corpse, examining the dead faces, especially of the monks, and during the night the report was brought back to the camp that I had disappeared.

Why did the Chinese do it? They ruined the Norbulingka believing that I was still inside it, so clearly they no longer cared whether they killed me or not. After they discovered I was not there, either alive or dead, they continued to shell the city and the monasteries. So they deliberately killed some thousands of our people, who were only armed with sticks and knives and a few short range weapons against artillery, and could not possibly have defended themselves or done any physical harm to the Chinese armies. We knew, as soon as we heard the dreadful news, that there was only one possible reason for it. Our people—not especially our rich or ruling classes, but our ordinary people—had finally, eight years after the invasion began, convinced the Chinese that they would never willingly accept their alien rule. So the Chinese were trying now to terrify them, by merciless slaughter, into accepting this rule against their will.

I can see now, in calm retrospect, that from that moment it was inevitable that I should leave my country. There was nothing more I could do for my people if I stayed, and the Chinese would certainly capture me in the end. All I could do was go to India and ask the Indian government for asylum, and devote myself there to keeping hope alive for my people everywhere. But that thought was so unwelcome that I still could not bring myself to accept it; and so we marched on toward Lhuntse Dzong, still with the hope, which only slowly died, that we could establish a center of government there.

🔳 12 🔳

INTO EXILE

So we went on, and our journey was even sadder than be-fore. I was young and strong, but some of my older com-panions were beginning to feel the effects of the long journey we had already made so quickly, and the most formidable part of it was still ahead.

But before we left Chongay, I had a most welcome chance to meet some more of the leaders of the Khampas and talk to them frankly. In spite of my beliefs, I very much admired their courage and their determination to carry on the grim battle they had started for our freedom, culture, and religion. I thanked them for their strength and bravery, and also, more personally, for the protection they had given me. I asked them not to be annoyed at the government proclamations which had described them as reactionaries and bandits, and told them exactly how the Chinese had dictated these and why we had felt compelled to issue them. By then, I could not in honesty advise them to avoid violence. In order to fight, they had sacrificed their homes and all the comforts and benefits of a peaceful life. Now they could see no alternative but to go on fighting, and I had none to offer. I only asked them not to use violence except in defending their position in the mountains. And I was able to warn them that our reports from Lhasa showed that the Chinese were planning to attack the part of the mountains where they were camped, so that as soon as they felt they could leave me they should go back to their defenses.

Many monk and lay officials were also waiting to see me there, but we had to cut our time short, because there was still every chance that the Chinese would come round by another route and cut us off before we were near enough to the frontier to have any way of retreat.

For another week we pressed on through the heart of the high mountains, and every day of that week we had to cross a pass. The snow had thawed in the valleys and on the lower passes, and the track was often slippery and muddy. But it sometimes led us to heights of over 19,000 feet, where the snow and ice were still lying. The route had been made by the tough mountain traders of old, and its stages were hard and long for people more used to the sheltered life of Lhasa.

The first night after Chongay we stayed in the monastery of which my Senior Tutor was high lama. The next day, we had to cross the Yarto Tag-la, which is particularly high and steep and difficult. Some of the ponies could not climb the track, and I and most of the others of the party had to dismount and lead them. But on the top, to our surprise, we found a fertile plateau where yaks were grazing, and a lake, thinly covered with ice, with a very high snow mountain to the north of it.

That night, after eleven hours of hard riding and climbing, very tired and saddle-sore, we reached a little place called E-Chhudhogyang. This place is so well known in Tibet that there is a proverb about it: "It's better to be born an animal in a place where there is grass and water than to be born in E-Chhudhogyang." It is a desolate spot, with a population of only four or five hundred. It is always in the grip of storms and gales, and the soil round it is ash-colored sand. So there was no cultivation at all, nor any grass or firewood. The people were almost destitute but happy, for they knew how to look poverty in the face. They welcomed us with open arms, and we were very grateful to share their humble homes. Some of my companions, who could not possibly be packed into the houses, were thankful for shelter in the cattle sheds.

By then we had been traveling for a week. Of course, I knew my friends abroad would be very concerned about the disorder in Lhasa and anxious to know what had happened to me; but none of us, as we struggled on, had any idea that our escape was in headlines in newspapers all over the world, and that people as far away as Europe and America were waiting with interest, and I hope I may say with sympathy, to hear whether I was safe. But even if we had known, there would have been nothing we could do about it, because of course we had no means of communicating with anyone.

But at that stage in our journey we heard that the Chinese had announced that they had dissolved our government, and that was something on which we could take action. Of course, they had no authority, legal or otherwise, to dissolve the government. In fact, by making that announcement they were breaking the only one of their promises in the Seventeen-Point Agreement which had so far nominally remained unbroken: the promise not to alter my status. But now that the announcement had been made, we thought there was some danger that Tibetans in isolated districts might think it had been made with my acquiescence. It seemed to us that the best thing to do was not simply to deny it, but to create a new temporary government; and we decided to do that as soon as we came to Lhuntse Dzong.

That was another two stages on. We left E-Chhudhogyang at five in the morning to face another high pass, the Tag-la, which took us up again, leading our ponies, above the snow-line. That was another hard day, ten hours of slippery, stony track before we reached a place called Shopanup; but there we all happily found accommodation, more comfortable than the night before, in a monastery.

The next day, we reached Lhuntse Dzong. A *dzong* is a fort, and Lhuntse Dzong is a vast building on a rock, rather like a smaller Potala. The officials and leaders of the place came out to receive us on the track as we approached, and as we came nearer we were welcomed by an orchestra of monks playing religious music from the terrace of the *dzong*. More than a thousand people, burning incense, stood at the sides of the road. We went into the *dzong* for a ceremony of thanksgiving for our safety.

After that we held the religious ceremony to consecrate the founding of the new temporary government. Monks, lay officials, village headmen, and many other people joined us on the second floor of the *dzong*, bearing the scriptures and appropriate emblems. I received from the monks the traditional emblems of authority, and the lamas who were present, including my tutors, chanted the enthronement prayers. When the religious ceremony was finished, we went down to the floor below, where my ministers and the local leaders were assembled. A proclamation of the establishment of the temporary government was read out to this assembly, and I formally signed copies of it to be sent to various places all over Tibet. The ceremonies ended with the staging of the Droshey, the Dance of Propitious Fortune.

We spent three hours in these pleasant ceremonies, and all of us quite forgot our immediate troubles and tragedies. We felt we were doing something positive for the future of Tibet.

From there, we also sent a letter to the Panchen Lama and offerings to his monastery of Tashi Lhunpo. By custom I ought to have sent these offerings at the time of my final examination a month or so before, but I had not been able to do it then.

But stories were still coming in of Chinese movements which sounded as though they were preparing to attack us, and so we moved on from the *dzong*, where we were very conspicuous, to a monastery a little farther on. There we held a meeting. By then, all of us had admitted the unwelcome truth to ourselves: that wherever we tried to stop in the mountains, the Chinese could hunt us out, and that my presence there could only lead in the end to more fighting, and more deaths of the brave men who would try to defend me. So at last we took the decision to send officials ahead of us to the border, with a message asking the Indian government for asylum. We did not want to cross the border before we had permission. We told them to press on into Indian territory and find the nearest Indian officials who could accept the message and send it on to Delhi. Then they should wait for an answer and bring it back to the frontier. This party left us at midnight to ride to the frontier with all the speed they could. In a straight line, it was about sixty miles to the point where we would have to cross it, and by the winding track it was probably double the distance.

We followed them at five o'clock in the morning. The nearer we rode to the frontier, the harder our journey became, and during the next few days we were beset by an extraordinary sequence of snowstorms, snow glare, and torrential rain. On that day the track divided and there were three possible routes to our next destination, which was a village called Jhora. I chose a route which involved another high pass, the Lagoe-la, and towards the top of it we ran into a heavy storm. It was very cold. Our fingers and hands were numbed and our eyebrows froze; my younger brother in particular had a very bad time of it; and those who had grown moustaches on the journey found them full of ice. But as we had no extra clothes, the only way to keep warm was to walk. So again we led our ponies. We tried to spare our ponies as much as we could all through our journey, not only because Tibetans always do, but especially because they had so far to go and there was so little fodder for them. That was one of the reasons why our journey took so long, and why our friends in other countries were left so long to wonder where we were.

By about eleven that morning we were clear of the pass and we stopped to rest. We had some bread, hot water and condensed milk, and it seemed delicious.

My three ministers and two tutors had gone another way, a little longer but with a lower pass, and some of the soldiers had been sent by the third of the alternatives. Nevertheless all of us except the two tutors managed to reach Jhora almost together, at three in the afternoon. The tutors came in a little later; and there we caught up at last with my mother and sister. They had taken a different route at a much earlier stage, and travelled so fast that they had been able to spend two days on the country estate which had been granted to my family at the time of my enthronement.

The people of Jhora gave us a warm welcome, and the next morning we started again at four o'clock, now in a long procession, two or three hundred of us, including the soldiers and the Khampas. For a little way, the track led along a valley bottom, but then it began to climb again towards the Karpo-la. The weather was fine and clear, but there was more snow there than we had seen before, and a strong wind was picking it up and whirling it into our faces. Very few of us had goggles to protect our eyes from the glare, and the others, to avoid snowblindness, had to cover their eyes with strips of colored cloth, or with the long braid of hair which many Tibetans wear round their heads.

Just beyond the top of that pass we heard a sound which in such a remote and barren place was unexpected, incongruous, and alarming. It was an aircraft. Suddenly the plane appeared, twin-engined, flying along our route. We were very conspicuous, hundreds of men and horses on the gleaming snow. Everyone dismounted and scattered. Most of the people crouched behind boulders—the soldiers unslung their rifles and were ready to fire if anything happened. I stood on a dark patch where the snow had blown away. The plane came straight over us, but it did not alter course, and it disappeared so quickly that we never saw what markings were on it.

Afterward we had long discussions about that plane, as people do when a sudden alarm is safely past. We thought it must have been Chinese, because no other nation would have sent a plane over that territory; and we thought it must have been looking for us, because even the Chinese could hardly have had any other purpose there. It gave no sign that we had been seen, and yet we could hardly believe that we had not. We went on with a rather uneasy feeling that the Chinese knew exactly where we were and which way we were going. But all we could do was divide into smaller parties, in case more aircraft were sent, perhaps to attack us. It was a confirmation that I must go into exile, and that any place where I stopped in Tibet would be likely to be bombed or besieged.

At about midday we stopped to rest and eat, and almost as soon as we sat down a duststorm broke over us. Discomforted, we went on, and immediately came to a very wide plain where the snow was lying thick. And there the sun came out brightly again, and those without goggles had a very hard time with the glare.

Two days more of this rather gruelling ride brought us to the last settlement in Tibet. Its name is Mangmang. And there we found waiting for us one of the officials who had gone on ahead, and he brought us the good news that the Indian government was willing to grant us asylum, and that he had actually seen preparations being made to receive us at Chhuthangmo, the first settlement where an Indian official was stationed.

That night at Mangmang we felt very safe. Most of the time until then we had been sleeping fully dressed except for our outer gowns. But Mangmang is in a corner of Tibet.

There is only one track leading to it, and that was well guarded, because we had left some hundreds of Khampas and soldiers at the last place where sidetracks joined our route. Now, unless they bombed us from the air, the Chinese could not take us by surprise or cut us off.

But there the weather did its worst for us. For the first time, we slept in tents, and it began to pour with rain. My tent had leaks in it. I woke up about three in the morning and tried to move my bed to a drier place. But that did not solve the problem, and I had to sit up for the rest of the night. Most of the others, in other tents, had the same kind of trouble. In the morning I was feeling very ill. We did not try to move on. I was too sick to ride, and during the day I grew worse.

My companions moved me to a small house but it was very dirty and black with smoke, and all the next night the cattle on the ground floor of the house underneath me were lowing and the cocks were crowing in the rafters above. So again I had very little sleep, and the next morning I could hardly move. While I was in that melancholy state, I heard a report from India on our radio that I had fallen off my horse and was badly injured. Except that I knew it would upset my friends, I was rather cheered up by that report— it was one misfortune, anyhow, that I had avoided so far.

Even if I had been well we might have had to wait a day at Mangmang, because I had to decide there who should come with me into India and who should be left behind. In the main, the religious and political officials came with me, and the military people stayed behind. The former had decided before we left Lhasa to follow me wherever I went, but the latter had come solely to protect me, and most of them wanted to turn back into Tibet to carry on the fight.

The second morning I was still too ill to ride a horse; yet we thought we ought to move, in order to relieve the rearguard of Khampas and soldiers of their responsibility. So my followers helped me onto the broad back of a *dzo,* the cross between a yak and a cow, which is an equable animal with an easy gait; and on that primeval Tibetan transport, I left my country.

There was nothing dramatic about our crossing of the frontier. The country was equally wild on each side of it, and uninhabited. I saw it in a daze of sickness and weariness and unhappiness deeper than I can express.

▣ 13 ▣

PRESENT AND FUTURE

Nobody could have remained quite despondent after the sympathy I received as soon as we reached the first villages and towns in India. We still had about a week's march, and several more mountain passes, before we came to a road or a railway. But on the way I was delighted to be met by an official I had known when I was in India before, and later by the liaison officer and the interpreter who had been with me on my previous visit. And then a very cordial telegram from Mr. Nehru was delivered to me. "My colleagues and I welcome you and send you greetings on your safe arrival in India," he said. "We shall be happy to afford the necessary facilities for you, your family, and entourage to reside in India. The people of India who hold you in great veneration will no doubt accord their traditional respect to your personage. Kind regards to you." And when we came down to the railway at Tezpur I was astonished and quite overwhelmed to find thousands of telegrams of good wishes and about 100 journalists and photographers, representing newspapers all over the world, who had come to that remote place to meet me and hear what they called "the story of the year." I was touched to know that so much interest had been taken in my fate, but at that moment I simply could not talk to them without reserve. My mind was not prepared for it, and it was a time when every word I said had to be thought over very carefully for the sake of my people still in Tibet. So I issued a statement giving an outline, in straightforward and carefully moderate terms, of the latter part of the story I have told in this book. The statement said how grateful I was for the messages of good will which had flooded in on me, and for the Indian government's welcome, and it added (it was written in the third person) that all the Dalai Lama wanted at the moment was to "express his sincere regret at the tragedy which has overtaken Tibet, and to hope fervently that these troubles will be over soon without any more bloodshed."

Two days later a statement was made in Peking which began: "The so-called statement of the Dalai Lama . . . is a crude document, lame in reasoning, full of lies and loopholes." After giving a description of events through Chinese Communist eyes, and insisting that I had been abducted by rebels from Lhasa, it said I was merely "reflecting the will of the imperialist aggressors," and suggested I had not issued the statement myself. During those days the Chinese also raged against "imperialists and Indian expansionists." It is so easy to wound with words, and so easy to seem superficially plausible if one has no regard for truth. Some sharp retorts were made by an Indian government spokesman, but I could not bring myself to enter an argument in which the Chinese were merely abusive. As for their reversals of the truth, I only made a second short statement to the press, a few days later, to say that I had indeed been responsible for the first, and stood by it.

It astonished me yet again to see how the Chinese blamed everybody they could think of for the revolt—like an injured dog which snaps at everybody. At different times they had tried to put the blame on the totally imaginary imperialists, the Tibetans who were living in India, the Indian government, and the "ruling clique" in Tibet, which was now their description of my government. They could not allow themselves to recognize the truth: that it was the people themselves, whom the Chinese claimed to be liberating, who had revolted spontaneously against their liberation, and that the ruling class of Tibet had been far more willing than the people to come to agreement.

Soon after I reached Tezpur the Indian government sent a special train to take us all to Mussoorie, in the foothills of the Himalayas, north of Delhi, where they had arranged for me to live temporarily. It was a journey of several days, and a memorable experience, because everywhere the train stopped enormous crowds had gathered to cheer us. I remembered the welcome of the Indian people on my previous visit, but now it had a new spontaneous fervor in it. It warmed my heart, and made me think of the Tibetan proverb: "Pain exists to measure pleasure by." Clearly they had not come just to look at me—they had come to show their sympathy for Tibet.

All the same, I was very glad to arrive at Mussoorie, and to be able to rest at last from that month of travel and mental strain, and to think over our problems in peace. I lived in Mussoorie for a year, until the Indian government offered me a bungalow which I could use as long as was necessary, at a place called Dharmsala in the extreme northwest of India, which is where I am living now.

Soon after I reached Mussoorie Mr. Nehru came to see me, and I was glad to have a long talk with him again. In June I made another statement to the press. Until then, I had said nothing harsh in public about the Chinese Communists, because I knew there was so much good in China, and could not bear to think that China would not negotiate reasonably. But refugees were pouring out of Tibet, and I was horrified at the stories they brought with them. I was forced to see that the Chinese had made up their minds to subdue Tibet by sheer brutality. I had to speak much more strongly. I said I thought the Peking government might not know exactly what their representatives were doing—indeed I still could not believe that Mao Tse-tung approved it. I suggested that if they would agree to let an international commission investigate the facts, I and my government would gladly accept its verdict. We were still willing to make a reasonable agreement, and indeed we shall always remain willing. But the Chinese never acknowledged that suggestion.

At that press conference I also formally repudiated the Seventeen-Point Agreement. I did that on my own initiative; but while I was at Mussoorie I had the chance, for the first time in my life, to meet experts on international law, and they confirmed that it was a proper thing to do.

Hitherto, the justice of our cause had seemed self-evident to me, but by now it was in my mind that if everything else failed we might have to ask the United Nations to consider our case. I was determined not to be hurried in that decision, but clearly intricate problems of law were becoming important. I knew the Chinese would claim that Tibet had always been part of China, in spite of our thirty-eight years of total freedom, and if they could substantiate that claim, they could also argue that their invasion of Tibet was a domestic matter in which the United Nations could not interfere.

But during my time at Mussoorie, the International Commission of Jurists examined the treaties of the early part of this century, as I have already explained, and concluded that we were a fully sovereign state, independent in fact and in law of Chinese control.

From that conclusion, the Commission went on to consider the Seventeen-Point Agreement. On the face of it, when we signed that agreement, we surrendered our sovereignty. We could argue that our representatives signed it under the threat of personal violence and further military action against Tibet. But it could be argued against us that to be forced to sign a treaty under duress does not always make the treaty voidable—treaties at the end of wars, for example, are signed under duress by the losers.

But if a treaty is violated by one of the parties to it, it can legally be repudiated by the other party, and then it is no longer in force. The Chinese had certainly violated the Seventeen-Point Agreement, and we were willing to prove it. Now I had repudiated the agreement, it had ceased to bind us, and our claim to sovereignty was the same as it had been before the agreement was signed.

There was another obvious difficulty in taking our case to the United Nations—neither of the parties in the dispute was a member. We were not because we had always cherished our isolation, and the Chinese were not because China was represented by the Chiang Kai-shek regime in Formosa. Nevertheless, I began to try to bring our case to the notice of the member nations.

The International Commission of Jurists was not acting for me or for Tibet—it does not act for governments or nations. It is an independent association of judges, lawyers, and teachers of law supported by 30,000 lawyers from fifty countries, and it exists to foster the rule of law and to mobilize world legal opinion whenever there seems to be a systematic violation of the rule of law. To my delight, the Commission began an energetic, objective study of events in Tibet, simply because it felt it had a duty to do so.

In its investigation, the Commission examined every Chinese and Tibetan statement, and sent its trained men to interrogate Tibetan refugees, and in doing so brought to light more horrors than even I had heard of. I do not think most people want to read of the extremes of cruelty, and I do not want to write of them, but in justice to my own people I must sum up the oppressions which that impartial inquiry revealed.*

Tens of thousands of our people have been killed, not only in military actions, but individually and deliberately. They

*The full statements accepted by the Commission, and its analysis and conclusions, are published in its reports: "The Question of Tibet and the Rule of Law" and "Tibet and the Chinese People's Republic" (International Commission of Jurists, Geneva, 1959 and 1960).

have been killed, without trial, on suspicion of opposing communism, or of hoarding money, or simply because of their position, or for no reason at all. But mainly and fundamentally they have been killed because they would not renounce their religion. They have not only been shot, but beaten to death, crucified, burned alive, drowned, vivisected, starved, strangled, hanged, scalded, buried alive, disemboweled, and beheaded. These killings have been done in public. The victims' fellow villagers and friends and neighbors have been made to watch them, and eye witnesses described them to the Commission. Men and women have been slowly killed while their own families were forced to watch, and small children have even been forced to shoot their parents.

Lamas have been specially persecuted. The Chinese said they were unproductive and lived on the money of the people. The Chinese tried to humiliate them, especially the elderly and most respected, before they tortured them, by harnessing them to ploughs, riding them like horses, whipping and beating them, and other methods too evil to mention. And while they were slowly putting them to death, they taunted them with their religion, calling on them to perform miracles to save themselves from pain and death.

Apart from these public killings, great numbers of Tibetans have been imprisoned and rounded up and taken away to unknown destinations, great numbers have died from the brutalities and privations of forced labor, and many have committed suicide in despair and misery. When men have been driven to take to the mountains as guerrillas, the women and children left in their villages have been killed with machine guns.

Many thousands of children, from fifteen years of age down to babies still at the breast, have been taken away from their parents and never seen again, and parents who protested have been imprisoned or shot. The Chinese either declared that the parents could work better without their children, or that the children would be sent to China to be properly educated.

Many Tibetan men and women believe the Chinese have sterilized them. They independently described a painful operation to the interrogators of the International Commission. The Commission did not accept their evidence as conclusive, because the operation did not correspond to any method of sterilization known to the medical profession in India. But on the other hand, there was no other explanation of it, and since the Commission's report was completed, new evidence has been given which has convinced me that the Chinese did sterilize all the men and women of a few villages.

Besides these crimes against the people, the Chinese have destroyed hundreds of our monasteries, either by physically wrecking them, or by killing the lamas and sending the monks to labor camps, ordering monks under pain of death to break their vows of celibacy, and using the empty monastic buildings and temples as army barracks and stables.

On all the evidence which they collected, the International Commission considered the Chinese guilty of "the gravest crime of which any person or nation can be accused"—that is, of genocide, "the intent to destroy, in whole or in part, a national, ethnical, racial or religious group as such." They were satisfied that the Chinese intend to destroy the Buddhists of Tibet.

In retrospect, I believe one can see the causes which led the Chinese to commit this crime.

In the beginning there were three reasons why they coveted Tibet. First, although our territory was large, there were only 7 or 8 million Tibetans and over 600 million Chinese, and their population was increasing by many millions every year. They often suffered from famine, and they wanted Tibet as extra living space. In fact, they have already settled hordes of Chinese peasants in Tibet, and I have no doubt they look forward to a time when Tibetans will be an insignificant minority. Meanwhile, Tibetan peasants are reduced to conditions worse than those of the peasants of the conquering race. There had never been famine in Tibet, in all its recorded history, but there is famine now.

Secondly, our country is certainly rich in minerals. We never exploited them because we had not enough desire for worldly riches. The Chinese claim great developments in Tibet, and I dare say their claims are true, but the developments are not for the benefit of Tibet, they are only for the enrichment of China.

Thirdly, the Chinese intend to dominate Asia, if not the world, as many of them frankly say, and the conquest of Tibet is a first step in this process. I am very far from being a military expert, but common sense suggests that no other country in Asia has the strategic importance of Tibet. With modern weapons, its mountains can be made an almost impregnable citadel from which to launch attacks on India, Burma, Pakistan, and the southeast Asian states, in order to dominate these countries, destroy their religions as ours is being destroyed, and spread the doctrine of atheism further. The Chinese are reported already to have built eighteen airfields in Tibet and a network of military roads through the country. Since they know perfectly well that India has no intention of attacking them, the only possible use for these military preparations is as a base for future expansion.

I believe now that the Chinese had all these aims more or less clearly in their minds when they first invaded Tibet ten years ago. Then they thought they could conquer Tibet with nothing much more than a pretence of legality and a threat of force; but the three aims, and especially the last, made it imperative for them to carry through their conquest even after they found how much it was going to cost them in materials and lives and guilt.

In the face of the destruction of my people and all that they live for, I devote myself in exile to the only courses of action left to me: to remind the world, through the United Nations, and now through this book, of what has happened and is happening in Tibet; to care for Tibetans who have escaped with me to freedom; and to plan for the future.

After I left my country, about sixty thousand Tibetans followed me into exile, in spite of the difficulty of finding a way of crossing the Himalayas and avoiding the Chinese guards. They did not come from any single class: they are really representative of our people. Among them are lamas of outstanding fame in our country, erudite scholars, about five thousand monks, some government officials, merchants and soldiers, and a great majority of humble peasants, nomads, and artisans. Many of them escaped by routes which were far more difficult and dangerous than mine. Some managed to bring their families; some children died of the hardships of the crossing of the mountains; but a great many men among them were separated from their families during the fighting, and have the added grief of knowing that their wives and children are abandoned to the Chinese.

These refugees are scattered now in communities in India, Bhutan, Sikkim, and Nepal. Some leading citizens of India, of all shades of opinion, have set up a Central Relief Committee for Tibetan Refugees, and they have been working in cooperation with the government of India to help our people. Voluntary relief organizations in many other countries have given help in money, or in food, clothes, or medicines. The governments of Britain, America, Australia, and New Zealand have sent gifts to help us educate our children, and the government of South Vietnam has sent us gifts of rice. We are very grateful indeed for all this kindness; it has been invaluable in helping us to begin to settle down. But of course we do not want to live on charity longer than we must; we want to stand on our own feet as soon as we can.

To this end, the government of India has helped to find work for most of our able-bodied men. At present, many of them, including a large number of monks, are working at building roads. But on the hot plains of India this is very unhealthy work for mountain people, and we are trying hard, with the sympathy of the government, to rehabilitate all our people in districts where the climate is not too different from our own. To this end, we have managed to establish training centers for handicrafts in Darjeeling and Dalhousie, both in the Himalayan foothills, where about six hundred people are learning useful trades. About four thousand are already installed as rural communities in Mysore and Assam—and other suitable places are being found. The rest of the older people are gradually finding work as farmers, and in forest clearance, and in dairy products; and we are training as many of our youngsters as possible, between the ages of sixteen and twenty-five in the mechanical knowledge which we lacked so completely in the old days.

The children have been a special anxiety to me—there are over five thousand of them under sixteen. It is even harder for children than for adults to be uprooted and taken suddenly to an entirely different environment, and many of them died in the early days from the change of food and climate. We had to do something drastic to preserve their health—and their education was also a matter of great importance. We know that our children in Tibet are being snatched away from their parents and brought up as Chinese Communists, not as Tibetan Buddhists. I have already told how Tibetan children refused to accept the Chinese creed; but it would be useless to think that children taken away as infants will not grow up as Communists—if Chinese communism lasts so long. So, in the next generation, the children in India may be very important people, a nucleus of the peaceful religious life which we wish to regain.

So far, we have established boarding schools in the foothills for about a thousand children, and we are preparing enough schools for them all. All the refugee parents are eager to send their children to these schools, where they can grow up healthy, and as true Tibetans. They are taught Tibetan, religious knowledge, and Tibetan history as their main subjects; and also English, Hindi, mathematics, geography, world history, and science.

The very small children below school age were another problem. It was they who suffered most of all from the climate of India, and the exposure to infections which hardly exist in Tibet. Their parents knew only too well that they could not look after them properly. So I offered them all my personal protection. I decided to set up a nursery and place it in the hands of my elder sister, and the government of India lent us two disused bungalows for the purpose near my present home at Dharmsala. The result was somewhat overwhelming. Almost before we knew where we were, 800 tiny children had been handed over to our care. My sister and her voluntary helpers had to improvise the barest necessities of life for this enormous family. We still cannot afford to give these little children the slightest luxury, but we can make sure that they are loved and kept healthy and happy—insofar as the children of refugees can ever be happy. The government of India is giving us rations for them, and other individuals and voluntary relief organizations are helping in many ways. Gradually, we have sent the older ones on to our other schools, and now at Dharmsala we have 300 children—all under seven.

It is for this kind of work, and to maintain a small nucleus of government, that the gold dust and silver bars which I deposited in Sikkim in 1950 have been so useful. I have sold them for cash, but they were not nearly enough for all the work that I and my government want to do and ought to do for our refugees and for the future of Tibet.

For me and for all the refugees, the pursuit of our religion remains just as important as the struggle to make our way materially in an unfamiliar world. We observe our ceremonies just as we did in Tibet, except, of course, that we cannot give them their ancient color and splendor. But perhaps, after all, they were too ornate in the old days, and it may not be a bad thing to observe them more austerely. I continue my own religious studies, besides learning English and reading as widely as I can, in order to bring myself more into touch with the modern world. I have repeated the pilgrimage to the holy places of India which was cut short by politics on my previous visit, and I have also been able to go to some of the sacred places of Christians, Hindus, and Jains, and to talk things over with men of these other religions; and I am happy to find how much we all have in common. During my pilgrimages to Budh Gaya and Benares, I ordained 162 Tibetan monks as Bhikshus, or full members of the monastic order. That was the first time I had performed the ceremony of ordination, and I reflected how fortunate I was to be able to do it in the very places where Lord Buddha had taught, at this time when his teaching was being persecuted in Tibet.

In these ways, with the help of many friends, life is being made tolerable for those who escaped with me. But, of course, the vast majority of Tibetans did not escape in time, and now they cannot escape. Behind the Himalayas, Tibet is like a gigantic prison camp. For them, the only thing I can do is try to see that they are not forgotten. Tibet is far away, and other countries have their own fears and troubles. We can well understand that there may be a tendency to let the events in Tibet drift back into history. Yet Tibet is on this very earth; Tibetans are human; in their way they are very civilized; certainly they are sensitive to suffering. I would dare to say that no people have suffered more since the Second World War; and their sufferings have not ended, they are continuing every day, and they will continue until the Chinese leave our country, or until Tibetans have ceased to exist as a race or as a religious community. So I have been persistent in reminding the world of our fate, by bringing our case before the United Nations.

I myself would not have known how to set about this task, nor would my Tibetan advisers; and at first the government of India tried to persuade me not to do it. But I went to Delhi and discussed it with the government and with the ambassadors of several other countries. Two members of the United Nations, Ireland and Malaya, sponsored our appeal, and it was discussed in the Steering Committee before the fourteenth session of the General Assembly in 1959. A vote was taken on the question of whether the General Assembly should consider Tibet—eleven voted in favor and five against, with four abstentions. But the Soviet delegation raised objections about the procedure of the meeting, and Czechoslovakia demanded a new vote. This time twelve were in favor and none against, and there were six abstentions.

So the matter was raised in the General Assembly, and finally this resolution was adopted:

> *The General Assembly,*
> *Recalling* the principles regarding fundamental human rights and freedoms set out in the Charter of the United Nations and in the Universal Declaration of Human Rights adopted by the General Assembly on 10 December 1948,
> *Considering* that the fundamental human rights and freedoms to which the Tibetan people, like all others, are entitled include the right to civil and religious liberty for all without distinction,
> *Mindful also* of the distinctive cultural and religious heritage of the people of Tibet and of the autonomy which they have traditionally enjoyed,
> *Gravely concerned* at reports, including the official statements of His Holiness the Dalai Lama, to the effect that the fundamental human rights and freedoms of the people of Tibet have been forcibly denied them,
> *Deploring* the effect of these events in increasing international tension and in embittering the relations between peoples at a time when earnest and positive

efforts are being made by responsible leaders to reduce tension and improve international relations,

1. *Affirms its belief* that respect for the principles of the Charter of the United Nations and of the Universal Declaration of Human Rights is essential for the evolution of a peaceful world order based on the rule of law;

2. *Calls* for respect for the fundamental human rights of the Tibetan people and for their distinctive cultural and religious life.

834th plenary meeting,
21 October 1959

Forty-five voted for this resolution, nine against, and twenty-six abstained.

I had hoped that the Chinese cared about international opinion, but this resolution had no noticeable effect on them. Nevertheless, it is always right to protest against injustice, whether or not the protest can stop the injustice; and we were encouraged that such a large majority of the representatives of the nations had supported our plea. It was only a pity that our case was regarded as part of the cold war. This is inevitable in the present state of the world, but really it should not be so. The invasion of Tibet was not fundamentally a Communist action. Earlier Chinese governments had invaded us or tried to do so; the Kuomintang government made an abortive attempt in the 1930s. The fact that China had turned to communism merely made the invasion more efficient and more ruthless, and more repellent to Tibetan people. But in the United Nations it also had the effect that other Communist powers felt obliged to vote in China's favor, although I cannot believe they all approved of China's action.

The support of this resolution gave me great satisfaction, but I did not feel I could let it rest at that. When the resolution was passed, the second report of the International

Commission of Jurists had not been issued, and the members of the General Assembly had not been told of the full extent of the Chinese atrocities, or of the Commission's conclusion that genocide was being committed in Tibet. So in 1960, with very valuable help from the Afro-Asian Council, the subject was put on the agenda of the General Assembly again, sponsored this time by Thailand and Malaya, with Ireland as co-sponsor. San Salvador also was willing to act as co-sponsor. But in that session, events in Africa took precedence; consideration of Tibet was postponed from day to day, and the Assembly adjourned before it had found time for our debate.

I shall continue to try to keep our case alive in the United Nations, because I believe the United Nations is the only source of hope for small oppressed nations, and indeed for the world. We must never allow a belief to grow up abroad that Tibet will ever acquiesce in Chinese Communist domination, for I know it never will.

Certainly Tibet will never be the same again, but we do not want it to be. It can never again be isolated from the world, and it cannot return to its ancient semifeudal system. I have told already of the reforms I had started to make before the Chinese stopped me; now in my exile, I have been carrying those reforms to their logical conclusion, with the help of experts on constitutional law, by drafting a new liberal and democratic constitution for Tibet, based on the principles of the doctrine of Lord Buddha and the Universal Declaration of Human Rights. This work is not finished yet. When it is, I shall submit it to an international committee of experts, and then to my people in exile, and as many of my people in Tibet as I can reach. Then I hope my people will elect a representative assembly and work out for themselves an interim constitution for the free country we all long to see.

My proposal will be for a parliament of a single house. The house should give full representation to the people as well as adequate representation for special interests. New laws should require a majority of the House, and constitutional amendments a three-quarters majority. The election should be made on the basis of universal adult suffrage, including the monks. This will present no difficulties in Tibet. Our population is small, and the people are intelligent. And although in the past our people took no interest in politics, they have certainly had to form their own opinions in the last ten years.

From time immemorial Tibet has been a unitary State, and a centralizing force will be all the more necessary in the new situation which the people and government of Tibet will have to face. I am against the establishment of any institution which might directly or indirectly promote conflicts amongst our people or tend to foster sectional or local interests at the expense of the national interest, for our primary purpose must always be that we should be one unified people.

I am advised that it would be better not to set up a parliamentary executive, but rather to adopt a presidential system, in which the Cabinet would be appointed, subject to safeguards, by the Dalai Lama as head of state. I shall therefore propose that the Dalai Lama should appoint his ministers, who would be free to address the parliament but not to vote; that parliament should be able to request the removal of a minister; and that if the Dalai Lama disagrees with parliament on this question, the decision of the Supreme Court should be binding on them both.

The Supreme Court should be appointed with safeguards similar to those applied to the Cabinet. The Dalai Lama himself should be subject to the deprivation of his powers, in the highest interests of the state, by legislative and judicial processes to be prescribed in the constitution.

During the minority of the Dalai Lama, or when he has ceased to exercise his power through death, disability, or deprivation, his place should be taken by a Regency Council of three or five members appointed by a two-thirds majority of parliament.

This constitution and its associated problems have been worked out in some detail now, but they are far from final, and even the outline I have given may be changed. Much more work remains to be done, and it also remains for the people of Tibet to approve it or express their own opinions. But I myself am convinced that government should always be by the will and through the cooperation of the people. I am ready to try to do whatever tasks my people ask of me, but I have no craving whatsoever for personal power or riches. I have no doubt at all that in this spirit, and under the guidance of our religion, we shall mutually solve whatever problems confront us, and make a new Tibet, as happy in the modern world as old Tibet was in its isolation.

All that is for the future. Looking at the past, I have no regret at all that I followed the policy of non-violence till the end. From the all-important point of view of our religion, it was the only possible policy, and I still believe that if my people had been able to follow it with me, the condition of Tibet would at least have been somewhat better now than it is. One might have compared our situation with that of a man arrested by the police although he has not committed any crime. His instinct may be to struggle, but he cannot escape; he is up against an overwhelming power; and in the end, it is better for him if he goes quietly, and puts his faith in the ultimate power of justice. But in Tibet, that simply could not be done. My people simply could not accept the Chinese or their doctrines, and their instinct to struggle could not be contained.

In spite of the atrocious crimes which Chinese have committed in our country, I have absolutely no hatred in my heart of the Chinese people. I believe it is one of the curses and dangers of the present age to blame nations for the crimes of individuals. I have known many admirable Chinese. I suspect there is nobody in the world more charming and civilized than the best of Chinese, and nobody more cruel and wicked than the worst. The atrocities in Tibet have been committed by Chinese of the lowest sort, soldiers and communist officials who were corrupted by the knowledge of having the power of life and death. Most Chinese would be bitterly ashamed if they knew of these deeds; but of course they do not know of them. We should not seek revenge on those who have committed crimes against us, or reply to their crimes with other crimes. We should reflect that by the law of Karma, they are in danger of lowly and miserable lives to come, and that our duty to them, as to every being, is to help them to rise toward Nirvana, rather than let them sink to lower levels of rebirth. Chinese communism has lasted twelve years; but our faith has lasted 2,500 years, and we have the promise of Lord Buddha that it will last as long again before it is renewed by the coming of another Buddha.

In these days of overwhelming military power all men and women can only live in hope. If they are blessed with peaceful homes and families, they hope to be allowed to keep them and to see their children grow up happily; and if they have lost their homes, as we have, their need for hope and faith is even greater. The hope of all men, in the last analysis, is simply for peace of mind. My hope rests in the courage of Tibetans, and the love of truth and justice which is still in the heart of the human race; and my faith is in the compassion of Lord Buddha.

Appendix I

AN OUTLINE OF THE BUDDHISM OF TIBET

The Need for Religion in Our Present Lives.

One reason for the pursuit of religion is that material progress alone will not give lasting pleasure or satisfaction. It seems, indeed, that the more we progress materially, the more we have to live under constant fear. Scientific technology has made marvelous advances, and no doubt will continue to develop. Man may reach the moon and try to exploit its resources for the advantage of human beings—the moon which some ancient believers regarded as the home of their god; and planets may also be conquered. Perhaps in the end, this progress will reveal potential enemies outside our world. But in any case, it cannot possibly bring ultimate and permanent pleasure to human beings, for material progress always stimulates desire for even further progress, so that such pleasure as it brings is only ephemeral. But on the other hand, when the mind enjoys pleasure and satisfaction, mere material hardships are easy to bear; and if a pleasure is derived purely from the mind itself, it will be a real and lasting pleasure.

No other pleasure can be compared with that derived from spiritual practice. This is the greatest pleasure, and it is ultimate in nature. Different religions have each shown their own way to attain it.

A second reason for the pursuit of religion is that we depend on religion even for the enjoyment of an appreciable amount of material pleasure. Pleasure and pain, in a general sense, do not arise only from external factors, but from internal factors as well. In the absence of the internal response, no amount of external stimulation can affect pleasure or pain. These internal factors are the after effects or impressions left on our minds by past actions; as soon as they come into contact with the external factors, we experience pleasure or pain again. An undisciplined mind expresses evil thoughts by evil actions, and those actions leave evil aftereffects on the mind; and as soon as external stimulation occurs, the mind suffers the consequences of its past actions. Thus, if we suffer miseries, they have their remote causes in the past. All pleasures and pains have their mental origins; and religions are required because without them, the mind cannot be controlled.

The Need of Religion for Our Future Lives.

How do we know that there is an afterlife? According to Buddhism, although the nature of cause and effect may be different, they must have the same essential properties, they must have a definite connection; otherwise the same cause cannot result in the same effect. For example, the human body can be perceived—it has form and color—and therefore, its immediate source or cause must also have these qualities. But mind is formless, and hence its immediate source or cause must also be formless. In analogy, the properties of the seeds of medicinal plants produce medicines, and the seeds of poisonous plants produce poison.

Most beings have physical bodies (though in some regions of existence beings have only minds). Both mind and body must have immediate sources. Both mind and body begin in this life as soon as conception occurs. The immediate source of a body is that of its parents. But physical matter cannot produce mind, nor mind matter. The immediate source of a mind must, therefore, be a mind which existed before the conception took place; the mind must have a continuity from a previous mind. This we hold to prove the existence of a past life. It has been demonstrated by the accounts of adults and children who remember their past lives—a phenomenon not only found in historical records but also observed today. On this basis, we can conclude that past life existed, and thence that future life will exist also. If belief in afterlife is accepted, religious practice becomes a necessity, which nothing else can supplant, in the preparation for one's future life.

One of the Many Religions of the World: Buddhism and Its Founder.

Just as a particular disease in the world is treated by various medical methods, so there are many religions to bring happiness to human beings and others. Different doctrines have been introduced by different exponents at different periods and in different ways. But I believe they all fundamentally aim at the same noble goal, in teaching moral precepts to mould the functions of mind, body, and speech. They all teach us not to tell lies, or bear false witness, or steal, or take others' lives, and so on. Therefore, it would be better if disunity among the followers of different religions could come to an end. Unity among religions is not an impossible idea. It is possible, and in the present state of the world, it is especially important. Mutual respect would be helpful to all believers; and unity between them would also bring benefit to unbelievers; for the unanimous flood of light would show them the way out of their ignorance. I strongly emphasize the urgent need of flawless unity among all religions. To this end, the followers of each religion should know something of other religions, and that is why I want to try to explain a little of the Buddhism of Tibet.

I must begin, however, by saying that it is very difficult to find exact English words to translate the philosophical terms of Buddhism which we use in Tibetan. It is hardly possible at present to find a scholar who has both a perfect knowledge of English and a perfect knowledge of Tibetan Buddhist philosophy and religion. Nor are there many authentic translations to consult. Books written or translated in the past have certainly done a great service to Buddhism, but some of them are rather rough translations, giving only superficial meanings. I hope that in the future this problem will be gradually solved, so that the more profound aspects of our religion can be understood in English. In the meantime, a very free translation is being used for this appendix, in order to make the English as simple as possible. I myself can only write of these matters with confidence in Tibetan, and have to rely on others, so far, for the precise choice of English words.

I have already explained in the course of my story that we Buddhists believe all beings are reborn, and strive, through a series of lives, toward the perfection of Buddhahood. We do not take it for granted that this perfection will be attained in a single lifetime, although it can be.

Of the mind and body of a man, we consider the mind superior; both speech and body are subject to it. Sins do not affect the intrinsic nature of mind. The essential mind is naturally pure. Sins are defects of peripheral or secondary minds. In the quest for enlightenment, these defects are removed one by one from the peripheral minds, and when no more defects remain in them, true perfection, or Buddhahood, is attained.

We believe that during the present Kalpa (aeon) a thousand incarnations of supreme Buddhas will come into this world. These Buddhas were living beings like ourselves before they attained perfection. They have the power to project reincarnations of their mind, body, and speech into millions of forms within a moment of time, in order to benefit all living beings in millions of worlds like ours. Each of these supreme incarnations will preach his own doctrine, and will work eternally for the salvation of all living beings.

We regard Lord Buddha, or Gautama Buddha, as he is also called, as one of these thousand Buddhas. He was born in a royal family in India over 2,500 years ago. In the early part of his life, he lived as a prince; but he became aware of cases of suffering which awakened him to the precariousness of human existence, so that he renounced his kingdom and turned to an ascetic life. From the limited point of view of ordinary beings, his life was marked by twelve main events: his descent from the heaven called Tushita, his conception, birth, schooling, marriage, renunciation, penance, meditation under the Bodhi tree (the tree of knowledge), defeat of Mara (the tempter), attainment of Buddhahood, preaching, and departure from Samsara (the round of existence).

His teaching differs from that of other Buddhas, for most of them preached only on Sutras (doctrinal treatises), but he also preached on Tantras (instructions in spiritual method).

After he attained Enlightenment, the Perfection of Buddhahood, at Budh Gaya, he preached three sermons, each at a different place in the part of India called Bihar. The first, at Varanasi (the modern Benares), was on the Four Noble Truths, about which I shall have more to say. It was mainly addressed to the Sravakas, meaning "hearers," who were people spiritually gifted but of limited outlook. The second sermon, at Girdhakuta, was about Shunyata (Voidness), the nonexistence of an ultimate self-nature, which I shall also mention again. This was addressed to Mahayanists, or followers of the Great Way, who were men of the highest intellect. The third sermon, at Vesali, was mainly meant for Mahayanists of somewhat less acute intellect.

Thus he not only preached on Sutras for Mahayanists and Hinayanists (followers of the Great and Lesser Ways, the two main schools of Buddhism), but also, after attaining the status of Vajra Dhara, that is to say on his initiation into the most profound methods, he preached many Tantras for Mahayanists. The great scriptures translated in Tibet under the title of Kangyur are all Lord Buddha's teachings.

Kangyur is divided into Sutra and Tantra. Sutra again is subdivided into three groups: Vinaya, which deals with teachings on moral codes; Sutantra on meditation; and Abhidharma on philosophical work concerning transcendental wisdom. These three subdivisions are called Tripitakas, and their fundamental principles are known in Sanskrit as Shila, Samadhi, and Prajnya. The Tantric part of Kangyur has four subdivisions. In Tibet these subdivisions of Tantra are sometimes included in the Sutantra division of the Sutra or Tripitaka.

The Spread of Buddhism in Tibet.

Before Buddhism was brought from India to Tibet, the bön religion was widespread in our country. It had originated in the neighboring country called Shang-Shung, and until recently there were still centers in Tibet where the followers of bön pursued deep study and meditation. In its beginning, I believe, it was not such a fruitful religion, but when Buddhism began to flourish in Tibet, bön also had an opportunity to enrich its own religious philosophy and meditational resources.

It was King Lho-Tho-Ri-Nyen-Tsen of Tibet who first introduced Buddhism to the country, well over a thousand years ago. It spread steadily, and in the course of time many renowned Pandits of India came to Tibet and translated texts of Sutras and Tantras with their commentaries.

This activity suffered a setback for some years during the

reign of the irreligious King Lang-Dar-Mar in the tenth Christian century; but that temporary eclipse was soon dispelled, and Buddhism revived and spread again, starting from the eastern and western parts of Tibet. Soon scholars, both Indian and Tibetan, were busy once more in translating religious works, and distinguished Pandits were visiting our country again for that purpose. But as Tibet began again to give birth to eminent native scholars, so, from that period, the numbers of scholars who came to Tibet from India and Nepal began gradually to diminish.

Thus, in what may be distinguished as the later period of Buddhism in Tibet, our religion developed separately from the later school of Indian Buddhism. But it remained exactly based on the teachings of Lord Buddha. In its essentials, it never suffered alterations or additions at the hands of Tibetan lamas. Their commentaries are clearly distinguished as commentaries, and they authenticated their work by constant references to the main teachings of Lord Buddha or the Indian Pandits.

For this reason, I cannot think it correct to regard Tibetan Buddhism as separate from the original Buddhism preached in India, or to call it Lamaism, as some people have. Certainly in minor matters there have been differences due to local conditions—as for example, the effect of climate on the habit worn by the religious. But I believe that a thorough study of the Tibetan language and Tibetan texts is essential now for anyone who would understand the entire teachings of Lord Buddha on both Sutras and Tantras.

Buddhism, as we have seen, was not brought to Tibet all at once; scriptures were introduced by different scholars at different times. In India during that period there were great Buddhist institutions, like Nalanda and Vikramasila Universities, which showed slight differences in their style of teaching, although they offered the same fundamental religion and philosophy. Consequently, separate groups grew into separate organizations or sects, all having the same basic tenets.

The most prominent of these Tibetan schools are the Nyingma, Kagyud, Sakya, and Geluk. Each of them adheres to all the teachings of Hinayana and Mahayana, including Tantrayana, for Tibetan Buddhists do not separate these teachings, but pay equal respect to them all. For moral guidance, they conform to the Vinaya rules which are principally followed by Hinayanists, while for more esoteric practices, of every degree of profundity, they use the methods of the Mahayana and Tantrayana schools.

The Meaning of Chös or Dharma.

The Tibetan word *Chös* is known as Dharma in Sanskrit, and it means "to hold." All the objects of this world which have definable identities of their own are known as Dharmas. Another meaning of Dharma is "to hold back from impending disaster," and it is in this sense that Dharma can mean "religion"; religion, that is to say, as opposed to secularism. Roughly speaking, any noble activities of mind, body, and speech are Dharma, or religion—which can save or hold one back from disaster. One is said to be practicing religion if one implements these activities.

The Four Noble Truths.

Lord Buddha said: "This is true suffering; this is true cause; this is true cessation; this is the true path." He also said: "Know the sufferings; give up their causes; attain the cessation of suffering; follow the true paths." Again he said: "Know the sufferings although there is nothing to know; relinquish the causes of misery although there is nothing to relinquish; be earnest in cessation although there is nothing to cease; practice the means of cessation although there is nothing to practice." These are three views of the intrinsic nature, action, and ultimate result of the Four Noble Truths. According to the Madhyamika theory (originally taught by Nagarjuna, a scholar of the third century of the Christian era), a theory which remains supreme among all the theories of different Buddhist schools, the explanation of these Truths is this:

True suffering means Samsara (the entire round of existence, of birth and rebirth), arising from Karma (that is, action and reaction) and from delusion.
True cause means Karma and delusion, which are the causes of true suffering.
True cessation means the complete disappearance of the preceding two truths.

The true path is the method by which cessation is achieved.

Thus the true cause of suffering leads to true suffering, but in following the true path, true cessation is achieved. Although this is the natural sequence, Lord Buddha preached the Four Truths by putting the effects first and the causes after. The reason for this was that if the suffering is known, the cause of it may be deduced; and when a strong desire to forsake the cause of suffering exists, means will be found to forsake it.

Samsara and Beings.

Samsara is the whole round of existence, and it with its miseries is the true suffering. To Samsara belongs everything which does not contain its own sufficient cause, everything which proceeds from a chain of other causes and thus is involved in Karma and delusion. Its essential nature is misery, and its function is to give a basis for the production of misery and to attract miseries for the future.

Spatially, Samsara is divided into three worlds—the Sensual World, the World of Form, and the Formless World. The beings in the first of these enjoy external sensual pleasures. The second of them, the World of Form, has two parts, in the lower of which the beings cannot enjoy external sensual pleasures but can enjoy undisturbed pleasure of internal contemplation. In the Formless World, the five sensual objects do not exist, nor do the five sensual organs to enjoy them; only a bare mind, void of distraction, exists and dwells entirely in a state of equanimity.

Samsara may also be divided according to the nature of the beings it contains, and by this means there are six divisions:

GODS These include beings in the world of celestial forms and of formless spirits, and the six kinds of gods found in the sensual world.

DEMI-GODS, OR TITANS These are like Gods in every respect except that they are mischievous.

HUMAN BEINGS

YI-DAG, OR PRETAS Living spirits who are afflicted constantly with the miseries of hunger and thirst.

ANIMALS

HELLS There are different grades of hells, and the living beings in each of them are also of various natures, according to their past Karma.

The Causes of the Miseries of Samsara.

The true causes of suffering are Karma and delusion.

Karma has been defined as "concordant action and reaction." According to the higher schools of Buddhism, it has two divisions, known in Tibetan as Sempai Lé and Sampai Lé. Sempai Lé is the initial stage of Karma in which physical action is yet to follow: the stage in which there is a subconscious impulse to act. Sampai Lé is the subsequent stage in which physical and oral action occurs. From the point of view of its results, there are three kinds of Karma. Meritorious Karma causes beings to take rebirth in the realms of gods, demi-gods, and men. Demeritorious Karma causes rebirth in the lower realms of animals, pretas and hells. Thirdly, Achala Karma, Invariable Karma, causes beings to take rebirth in the upper worlds, Rupa and Arupa Dhatu, a world of form and a formless world. The results of Karma may be experienced in this present life, or in the next life, or in subsequent lives.

Delusion is not a part of the essential or central mind, which, as I have said, is intrinsically pure: it is a defect of one of the peripheral or secondary minds. When this secondary mind is stimulated, delusion becomes influential, dominating the central mind and causing sin.

There are very many kinds of delusion: passion, anger, pride, hatred, hostility and so on. Passion and hostility are the main delusions: by passion we mean a passionate attachment to men or things. Passion may become self-attachment or egoism, and from it one may develop pride through a sense of superiority; or, on encountering hostility toward oneself, one may develop a counter-hatred. Again, through ignorance and lack of understanding, one may be led to oppose the truth. This strong "I-consciousness" has been fostered in all beings in Samsara since time immemorial, and they are so habituated to it that they experience it even in their dreams.

In fact, all cognizable things are empty from their very nature, but through delusion they appear as self-originating and self-sufficing entities. Conversely, this distorted conception is at the root of all delusion.

The Essence of Nirvana.

Samsara, in another sense, implies a bondage. Nirvana implies a liberation from this bondage: the true cessation, the third of the Noble Truths. I have explained that the causes of Samsara are Karma and delusion. If the roots of delusion are thoroughly extracted, if creation of new Karma to cause rebirth in the Samsara is brought to an end, if there are no more delusions to fertilize the residual Karmas of the past, then the continual rebirth of the suffering being will cease. But such a being will not cease to exist. It has always existed in a body with a mortal residue, a body given birth by previous Karma and delusion. But after the cessation of rebirth, after the liberation from Samsara and the achievement of Nirvana, it will continue to have consciousness and a spiritual body free of delusion. This is the meaning of the true cessation of suffering.

Nirvana can indicate a lower stage, in which there is simply no suffering, and also it can mean the highest stage, called Mahaparinirvana. This is the stage of supreme Enlightenment, total and unqualified, free from all moral and mental defilement, and from the defilement caused by the power of discriminative thought: the stage of Buddhahood.

Hinayana.

A prescribed path must be followed to attain either of the states of Nirvana described above: the true path, the fourth of the Noble Truths. Hinayana and Mahayana represent two schools of thought concerning this path. Hinayanists, the followers of the Lesser Way, basically seek to attain Nirvana for the individual's own sake. According to this school, the mind should have a strong will to renounce Samsara; it should pursue religious ethics (Sila), and simultaneously practice concentration (Samadhi) and meditation (Vipessana, *Tibetan:* Lhag-thong), so that delusion and the seeds of delusion may be purged, and may not grow again. Thus Nirvana is attained. The paths to be followed include the Paths of Preparation, of Application, of Seeing, of Practice, and of Fulfillment.

Mahayana.

Mahayanists aim at attaining the highest stage of Nirvana, Buddhahood, for the sake not only of the individual but of all other sentient beings. Motivated by the thought of Enlightenment (Bodhichitta) and by compassion, they follow almost the same paths as those of Hinayana. But in addition to those paths, they practice other methods (Upayas) such as the six Paramitas (transcendent virtues). By this practice, Mahayanists seek not only to rid themselves of delusion but also of the defilement of sin, and thus to attain Buddhahood. The five Mahayanic paths are likewise known as the Paths of Preparation, Application, Seeing, Practice and Fulfillment. But although the names of the paths are the same as those of Hinayana, there is a qualitative difference between them. And since Mahayanists have a different fundamental motive and in general follow different paths and practice different methods, the final goal which they achieve is different.

The question is sometimes asked whether Hinayanists, having achieved Nirvana, will be confined to the stage they have attained, or whether they will subsequently follow the Mahayana. The answer must be that they will not regard their own stage of Nirvana as the final goal, but will certainly then adopt ways to attain Buddhahood.

Tantrayana.

The paths I have mentioned are doctrinal paths, and they must be followed to provide a sound foundation before Tantrayana (the way of Yogic Method) is practiced. In Tibet, the greatest care was taken before any Tantric doctrine was introduced. Spiritual teachers always investigated whether the doctrine was among those preached by Lord Buddha, and submitted it to logical analysis by competent Pandits, and also tested its effects in the light of experience, before confirming its authenticity and adopting it. This was necessary because there are many non-Buddhist Tantric doctrines which were apt to be confused with those of Buddhism because of superficial resemblances.

The Tantrayana falls into four classes, and it has a vast number of treatises which cannot be enumerated here. In the simplest terms, this is its system: as already explained, bad Karmas are held responsible for the various kinds of miseries we suffer. These bad Karmas are created through delusion. Delusion is essentially due to an undisciplined mind. The mind should therefore be disciplined and trained by stopping the flow of evil thought. This flow may be stopped, and the wandering or projecting mind brought to rest, by concentration on the physical makeup of one's body and the psychological makeup of one's mind.

The mind may also be focussed on external objects of

contemplation. For this, strong contemplative powers are needed, and the figures of deities are found to provide the most suitable objects. For this reason, there are many images of deities in Tantrayana. These are not arbitrary creations. Images, as objects of contemplation to purify the body, mind, and senses have to be created in wrathful as well as peaceful aspects, and sometimes with multiple heads and hands, to suit the physical, mental, and sensual aptitudes of different individuals in striving for the final goal.

Progress towards this goal is achieved in some cases mainly through a strong power of faith and devotion, but in general it is achieved by the power of reason. And if the transcendental path is systematically followed, reason will provide in the course of it many causes for heartfelt belief.

Dual Truth.

Every religious path has a Wisdom (Prajna) and a Method (Upaya).

Wisdom is concerned with Absolute Truth (Paramarthasatya), and Method with Relative Truth (Sambrithsatya). Nagarjuna has said: "Dharmas revealed by the Buddhas are always fully in accordance with the Dual Truths, both Absolute and Relative Truth."

When the final end, Buddhahood, is achieved, an individual acquires two forms of Buddha Kayas or Bodies. These two Kayas are the effects of his practice of Wisdom and Method in following the doctrinal paths; and his Wisdom and Method are the results of the two truths which provide the universal basis. An understanding of the Dual Truths is therefore very important, but it involves some difficulties. Different schools of Buddhist thought hold different views concerning these truths. According to Uma Thal Gyurpa (the theory of Madhyamaka held by the Prasangika School of Buddhism), things we perceive with our senses have two aspects—perceptible and imperceptible. Roughly speaking, Relative Truth is concerned with the knowledge of things and of mental concepts in their perceptible aspects, and Absolute Truth with knowledge of their imperceptible aspects.

Universal Voidness and True Cessation are Absolute Truths; all else is relative.

Outline of the Method of Following Buddhism.

The perfect practice of Buddhism is not achieved merely through superficial changes, for example through leading a monastic life or reciting from holy books. It is even open to question whether these activities in themselves should be called religious or not; for religion should be practiced in the mind. If one has the right mental attitude, all actions of body and speech can become religious. But if one lacks the right attitude, if one does not know how to think properly, one will achieve nothing even by spending the whole of one's life in monasteries and in reading from the scriptures. So that proper mental attitude is the first essential. One should take the Three Jewels—Buddha, Dharma, and Sangha—as one's final refuge; one should observe the laws of Karma and its fruits; and one should cultivate thoughts of benefit to other beings.

If religion is earnestly followed by renouncing the world, it brings great joy to its follower. There are many people in Tibet who have renounced the world in this way, and they gain an indescribable mental and physical satisfaction. The sum total of worldly pleasure, gained through the motive of self-love and the struggle to fulfill that love, is not comparable to a fraction of it. Such people are also of the greatest benefit to others, by virtue of their own inward state, which enables them to diagnose not only the true causes but also the true remedies of the ills of mankind. And yet this renouncing of the world is not possible for everybody, because the sacrifices it demands are very great.

What sort of Dharma, what sort of religion, can then be prescribed for people in ordinary walks of life? Immoral worldly activities, of course, are to be ruled out; these activities are never compatible with any religion. But morally justifiable activities, such as helping to administer the government of a country, or indeed anything useful and productive, any steps towards promoting the pleasure and happiness of others, can certainly go together with the practice of Dharma. Kings and ministers of India and Tibet have promoted Dharma. Salvation can be achieved, if one truly seeks for it, merely in leading a household life. But there is a saying: "People who make no mental effort, even if they remain in retreats in the mountains, like animals hibernating in their holes, only accumulate causes for descending into hell."

Perhaps I may conclude with an old Tibetan story:

Once long ago there was a famous lama whose name was Drom. One day he saw a man walking around a stupa. "Look," he said, "it is quite a good thing that you walk around a stupa. But it would be better to practice religion."

"Well, I had better read a holy book then," the man said to himself. And so he started laboriously reading from a book till one day Drom happened to see him again.

"Reading from a holy book is no doubt very good," Drom said, "but it would be better still if you would practice religion."

And the man thought: "Even recitation is no good. How about meditation?"

Before long, Drom saw him in meditation and said: "It is no doubt very good to meditate. But it would really be better if you would practice religion."

"Pray, what then do you mean by practicing religion?" the bewildered man replied.

"Turn your mind away from the forms of this worldly life," Drom told him. "Turn *your mind* towards religion."

Appendix II

APPEALS BY HIS HOLINESS THE DALAI LAMA OF TIBET TO THE UNITED NATIONS

DOCUMENT A/1549.

November 11, 1950, Kalimpong

The attention of the world is riveted on Korea where aggression is being resisted by an international force. Similar happenings in remote Tibet are passing without notice. It is in the belief that aggression will not go unchecked and freedom unprotected in any part of the world that we have assumed the responsibility of reporting to the United Nations Organization, through you, recent happenings in the border area of Tibet.

As you are aware, the problem of Tibet has taken on alarming proportions in recent times. This problem is not of Tibet's own making but is largely the outcome of unthwarted Chinese ambition to bring weaker nations on its periphery under its active domination. Tibetans have for long lived a cloistered life in their mountain fastnesses, remote and aloof from the rest of the world, except in so far as His Holiness the Dalai Lama, as the acknowledged head of the Buddhist Church, confers benediction and receives homage from followers in many countries.

In the years preceding 1912, there were indeed close friendly relations of a personal nature between the Emperor of China and His Holiness the Dalai Lama. The connection was essentially born of belief in a common faith and may correctly be described as the relationship between a spiritual guide and his lay followers; it had no political implications. As a people devoted to the tenets of Buddhism, Tibetans had long eschewed the art of warfare, practiced peace and tolerance, and for the defense of their country relied on its geographical configuration and on noninvolvement in the affairs of other nations. There were times when Tibet sought but seldom received the protection of the Chinese Emperor. The Chinese, however, in their natural urge for expansion, have wholly misconstrued the significance of the ties of friendship and interindependence that existed between China and Tibet as between neighbors. To them China was suzerain and Tibet a vassal State. It is this which first aroused legitimate apprehension in the mind of Tibet regarding China's designs on its independent status.

The conduct of the Chinese during their expedition of 1910 completed the rupture between the two countries. In 1911–1912, Tibet, under the Thirteenth Dalai Lama, declared its complete independence—even Nepal simultaneously broke away from allegiance to China—while the Chinese revolution of 1911, which dethroned the last Manchurian Emperor, snapped the last of the sentimental and religious bonds that Tibet had with China. Tibet thereafter depended entirely on its isolation, its faith in the wisdom of the Lord Buddha, and occasionally on the support of the British in India for its protection. No doubt in these circumstances the latter could also claim suzerainty over

Tibet. Tibet, notwithstanding Anglo-Chinese influence from time-to-time, maintained its separate existence, in justification of which it may be pointed out that it has been able to keep peace and order within the country and remain at peace with the world. It continued to maintain neighborly good will and friendship with the people of China, but never acceded to the Chinese claim of suzerainty in 1914.

It was British persuasion which led Tibet to sign a treaty which superimposed on it the nominal (noninterfering) suzerainty of China and by which China was accorded the right to maintain a mission in Lhasa, though it was strictly forbidden to meddle in the internal affairs of Tibet. Apart from that fact, even the nominal suzerainty which Tibet conceded to China is not enforceable because of the nonsignature of the treaty of 1914 by the Chinese. It will be seen that Tibet maintained independent relations with other neighboring countries, such as India and Nepal. Furthermore, despite friendly British overtures, it did not compromise its position by throwing in its forces in the Second World War on the side of China. Thus it asserted and maintained its complete independence. The treaty of 1914 still guides relations between Tibet and India, and China not being a party to it may be taken to have renounced the benefits that would have otherwise accrued to it from the treaty. Tibet's independence thereby reassumed *de jure* status.

The slender tie that Tibet maintained with China after the 1911 revolution became less justifiable when China underwent a further revolution and turned into a full-fledged Communist State. There can be no kinship or sympathy between such divergent creeds as those espoused by China and Tibet. Foreseeing future complications, the Tibetan Government broke off diplomatic relations with China and made a Chinese representative in Lhasa depart from Tibet in July, 1949. Since then, Tibet has not even maintained formal relations with the Chinese Government and people. It desires to live apart, uncontaminated by the germ of a highly materialistic creed, but China is bent on not allowing Tibet to live in peace. Since the establishment of the People's Republic of China, the Chinese have hurled threats of liberating Tibet and have used devious methods to intimidate and undermine the Government of Tibet. Tibet recognizes that it is in no position to resist. It is thus that it agreed to negotiate on friendly terms with the Chinese Government.

It is unfortunate that the Tibetan mission to China was unable to leave India through no fault of its own, but for want of British visas, which were required for transit through Hong Kong. At the kind intervention of the Government of India, the Chinese People's Republic condescended to allow the Tibetan mission to have preliminary negotiation with the Chinese Ambassador to India, who arrived in New Delhi only in September. While these negotiations were proceeding in Delhi, Chinese troops, without warning or provocation, crossed the Di Chu river, which has for long been the boundary of Tibetan territory, at a number of places on October 7, 1950. In quick succession, places of strategic importance such as Demar, Kamto, Tunga, Tshame, Rimochegotyu, Yakalo and Markham, fell to the Chinese. Tibetan frontier garrisons in Kham, which were maintained not with any aggressive design, but as a nominal protective measure, were all wiped out. Communist troops converged in great force from five directions on Chamdo, the capital of Kham, which fell soon after. Nothing is known of the fate of a minister of the Tibetan Government posted there.

Little is known in the outside world of this sneak invasion. Long after the invasion had taken place, China announced to the world that it had asked its armies to march into Tibet. This unwarranted act of aggression has not only disturbed the peace of Tibet, but it is also in complete disregard of a solemn assurance given by China to the Government of India, and it has created a grave situation in Tibet and may eventually deprive Tibet of its long-cherished independence. We can assure you, Mr. Secretary-General, that

Tibet will not go down without a fight, though there is little hope that a nation dedicated to peace will be able to resist the brutal effort of men trained to war, but we understand that the United Nations has decided to stop aggression whenever it takes place.

The armed invasion of Tibet for the incorporation of Tibet in Communist China through sheer physical force is a clear case of aggression. As long as the people of Tibet are compelled by force to become a part of China against their will and consent, the present invasion of Tibet will be the grossest instance of the violation of the weak by the strong. We therefore appeal through you to the nations of the world to intercede in our behalf and restrain Chinese aggression.

The problem is simple. The Chinese claim Tibet as a part of China. Tibetans feel that racially, culturally, and geographically they are far apart from the Chinese. If the Chinese find the reactions of the Tibetans to their unnatural claim not acceptable, there are other civilized methods by which they could ascertain the views of the people of Tibet; or, should the issue be purely juridical, they are open to seek redress in an international court of law. The conquest of Tibet by China will only enlarge the area of conflict and increase the threat to the independence and stability of other Asian countries.

We Ministers, with the approval of His Holiness the Dalai Lama, entrust the problem of Tibet in this emergency to the ultimate decision of the United Nations, hoping that the conscience of the world will not allow the disruption of our State by methods reminiscent of the jungle.

> The Kashag (Cabinet) and National Assembly of Tibet, Tibetan delegation, Shakabpa House, Kalimpong.
>
> Dated Lhasa, the twenty-seventh day of the ninth Tibetan month of The Iron Tiger Year (November 7, 1950).

New Delhi
September 9, 1959

His Excellency Secretary General
United Nations
New York

Your Excellency,

Kindly refer to the proceedings of the General Committee of the United Nations General Assembly held on Friday, November 24, 1950, at which it was resolved that the consideration of El Salvador's complaint against "invasion of Tibet by foreign forces" should be adjourned in order to give the parties the opportunity to arrive at a peaceful settlement. It is with the deepest regret that I am informing you that the act of aggression has been substantially extended with the result that practically the whole of Tibet is under the occupation of the Chinese forces. I and my Government have made several appeals for peaceful and friendly settlement, but so far these appeals have been completely ignored. Under these circumstances, and in view of the inhuman treatment and crimes against humanity and religion to which the people of Tibet are being subjected, I solicit immediate intervention of the United Nations and consideration by the General Committee on its own initiative of the Tibetan issue, which had been adjourned. In this connection I and my Government wish to emphasize that Tibet was a sovereign State at the time when her territorial integrity was violated by the Chinese armies in 1950. In support of this contention the Government of Tibet urges the following:

First, no power of authority was exercised by the Government of China in or over Tibet since the Declaration of Independence by the Thirteenth Dalai Lama in 1912.

Second, the sovereign status of Tibet during this period finds conclusive evidence in the fact that the Government of Tibet concluded as many as five international agreements immediately before and during these years.

Third, the government of Tibet takes its stand on the Anglo-Tibet Convention of 1914 which recognized the sovereign status of Tibet and accorded the same position to the Tibetan plenipotentiary as was given to the representatives of Great Britain and China. It is true that this convention imposed certain restrictions on the external sovereignty of Tibet, but these did not deprive her of her internal position. Moreover, these restrictions ceased to have any effect on the transfer of power in India.

Fourth, there is no valid and subsisting international agreement under which Tibet or any other power recognized Chinese suzerainty.

Fifth, the sovereign status of Tibet is equally evident from the fact that during the Second World War Tibet insisted on maintaining her neutrality and only allowed the transport of nonmilitary goods from India to China through Tibet. This position was accepted by the Governments of Great Britain and China.

Sixth, the sovereign status has also been recognized by other powers. In 1948 when the Trade Delegation from the Government of Tibet visited India, France, Italy, the United Kingdom, and the United States of America, the passport issued by the Tibetan Government was accepted by the governments of these countries.

Your Excellency, I and my government also solicit immediate intervention of the United Nations on humanitarian grounds. Since their violation of the territorial integrity of Tibet, the Chinese forces have committed the following offenses against the universally accepted laws of conduct:

First, they have dispossessed thousands of Tibetans of their properties, and deprived them of every source of livelihood, and thus driven them to death and desperation.

Second, men, women, and children have been pressed into

labor gangs and made to work on military constructions without payment or on nominal payment.

Third, they have adopted cruel and inhuman measures for the purpose of sterilizing men and women with view to the total extermination of the Tibetan race.

Fourth, thousands of innocent people of Tibet have been brutally massacred.

Fifth, there have been many cases of murder of leading citizens of Tibet without any cause or justification.

Sixth, every attempt has been made to destroy our religion and culture. Thousands of monasteries have been razed to the ground and sacred images and articles of religion completely destroyed. Life and property are no longer safe, and Lhasa, the capital of the State, is now a dead city. The sufferings which my people are undergoing are beyond description, and it is imperatively necessary that this wanton and ruthless murder of my people should be immediately brought to an end. It is under these circumstances that I appeal to you and the United Nations in the confident hope that our appeal will receive the consideration it deserves.

The Dalai Lama

Swargashram,
Dharmsala, Cantt.
East Punjab, India
September 2, 1960

His Excellency
Dag Hammarskjöld,
Secretary General of the United Nations,
New York

Your Excellency:
    Last year when I formally appealed to Your Excellency

for the intervention of the United Nations on behalf of the people of Tibet, Your Excellency was kind enough to help my representatives with your inestimable advice and valuable support. I have, therefore, ventured to approach you once again in the name of the people of Tibet who are today groaning under an intolerable burden of terror and tyranny.

As Your Excellency is no doubt aware, the situation in Tibet has now become a grim tragedy. Hundreds of Tibetans have been arriving in India and Nepal to escape from merciless persecution and inhuman treatment. But there are thousands of others who find it impossible to seek asylum in the neighboring countries and are, therefore, threatened with immediate death and destruction. I feel most strongly that something must be done immediately to save the lives of these innocent men, women, and children, and have accordingly sought the assistance and support of the governments of many member States of the United Nations. His Excellency the Prime Minister of the Federation of Malaya, and the Government of Thailand have generously responded to my appeal and have declared their intention to raise the Tibetan question at the next session of the General Assembly of the United Nations. It is in this connection that I have ventured to approach Your Excellency once again. As on the last occasion, I trust Your Excellency will find it possible to use your good offices and influence in devising a practical solution to the tragic problem of Tibet. Your Excellency, I hope, will permit me to express my own feelings in the matter. I firmly believe that the only effective and speedy way in which the United Nations can help the unfortunate people of Tibet is by way of mediation, either through an *ad hoc* body appointed for the purpose by the General Assembly or through Your Excellency's good offices. This is what I feel, and have also expressed this view to His Excellency Tunku Abdul Rahman and His Excellency Marshal Sarit Thanarat. This, however, is only a suggestion I am making for Your Excellency's consideration, and I would be most grateful if Your Excellency could see your way to favor me with your personal advice.

With assurances of my highest esteem and consideration.

I remain,
The Dalai Lama.

Swargashram,
Dharmsala, Cantt.
East Punjab, India
September 20, 1960

His Excellency
Dag Hammarskjöld
Secretary-General,
United Nations,
New York, N. Y.

Your Excellency:

May I convey to the United Nations and to Your Excellency my warm appreciation of the great work which has been and is being done in Congo under the auspices of the U.N.

2. Kindly refer to my letter of September 9, 1959, circulated by you as Note No. 2033, and also to my letter to Your Excellency of September 2, 1960.

3. I am happy to learn that the Question of Tibet has been inscribed on the agenda of the U.N. Assembly for this year at the instance of Malaya and Thailand to whom I am deeply grateful. I do hope that all the peaceloving countries will take heed of the voice of my people and provide for them a ray of light in the night of subjugation and oppression through which they are passing.

4. I am happy to note that in his speech in the Assembly on September 24, 1960, H.E.N. Krushchev called for the freedom of all colonial peoples. Unfortunately my country

has been reduced to the status of a colonial country, and I hope that along with other countries the USSR will also raise its powerful voice in support of the restoration of freedom to my country.

5. I assert that long before 1911–12 there was no vestige of Chinese authority in Tibet, but it is not necessary for me to examine the historical aspect of this question for the purposes of this appeal.

6. Whatever the position of Tibet may have been prior to 1911–12, in any event, from the day that the Thirteenth Dalai Lama proclaimed the independence of Tibet, after the invading Chinese armies had been driven out of Tibet, Tibet was not only independent *de facto* but *de jure*.

7. In 1913 the Tibetan Government entered into a treaty with the Government of Mongolia. This treaty was entered into under the authority of the Dalai Lama. By this treaty Tibet and Mongolia declared that they recognized each other as independent countries.

8. With a view to settle some outstanding questions, Tibet agreed to enter into tripartite discussions which commenced in 1913, at Simla. The parties to the discussion were the British Government, Chinese Government, and Tibetan Government. The representative of each government being a plenipotentiary on behalf of his government. This appears clearly from the text of the Convention which was initialed by the representatives of all the parties.

9. This fact is also emphasized by the White Paper No. 11 issued by the Government of India (page 38) entitled "Notes, Memoranda, and Letters Exchanged between the Governments of India and China, September–November 1959." This has been further emphasized in the note of the Government of India dated February 12, 1960 (pp. 94, 95) in the White Paper No. III issued by the Government of India.

10. Although the text of the Convention was initialed by the representative of the Chinese Government, the Chinese Government backed out and ultimately on the third of July, 1914, the signatures on behalf of the Dalai Lama, in his capacity as the head of the Tibetan State, and the British plenipotentiary were appended. At the same time the plenipotentiaries of Great Britain and Tibet, in view of the refusal of the Chinese Government, signed the following Declaration:

11. "We the plenipotentiaries of Great Britain and Tibet, hereby record the following declaration to the effect that we acknowledge the annexed Convention as initialed to be binding on the governments of Great Britain and Tibet, and we agree that so long as the Government of China withholds signature to the aforesaid Convention, she will be debarred from the enjoyment of all privileges accruing therefrom.

12. "In token whereof we have signed and sealed this declaration, two copies in English and two in Tibetan.

13. "Done at Simla this third day of July, A.D. 1914, corresponding with the Tibetan date—the tenth day of the fifth month of The Wood Tiger Year.

A. Henry McMahon,
British Plenipotentiary

(Seal of the British Plenipotentiary)
(Seal of the Dalai Lama)
(Seal of the Lonchen Shatra) *(Signature of the Lonchen Shatra)*
(Seal of the Drepung Monastery)
(Seal of the Gaden Monastery)
(Seal of the National Assembly)"

14. The Chinese Government, never having adhered to the terms of the Convention, never became entitled to any of the advantages which they may have derived from the terms of the Convention.

15. In 1926 Tibet was represented at a Boundary Commission consisting of the representatives of Tibet, Tehri, and Great Britain which met at Nilang.

16. Between 1912 and 1950 there was not even a semblance of Chinese authority in Tibet. There was a Chinese mission in Tibet which arrived in 1934 to offer condolences on the death of the Thirteenth Dalai Lama. This Mission was permitted to continue to stay in Tibet on the same footing as the missions from Nepal and from the Government of India.

17. On numerous occasions after 1936 the officers of the Chinese mission to Lhasa used to travel via India to Tibet. On every occasion the Indian Government granted or refused transit visas after consulting the wishes of the Government of Tibet.

18. In 1949 even this mission was expelled from Tibet.

19. Tibet was not a party to the Sino-Japanese war, and even during the Second World War Tibet insisted on its position as a neutral and did not permit the transport of war material from India to China.

20. The Chinese claim that Tibetan delegates participated in the Constituent Assembly in 1946 and that they also sat in the Chinese National Assembly in 1948. This claim is absolutely false. Dzasak Khemey Sonam Wangdo, who was the leader of the Delegation which went to China says, "In 1946 the Tibetan Government had sent a good will Mission headed by Dzasak Rongpel-Ihun, Thubten Samphel and myself Dzasak Khemey Sonam Wangdo with assistants to offer victorious greetings to Britain, America, and the Kuomintang Government; we traveled via Calcutta to New Delhi, and offered the greetings to Britain and America through their Ambassadors; from there we went by air to Nanking and offered greetings. Due to illness and medical treatment we remained there for a few months. Then we toured several provinces and on our return to Nanking they were having their big as-

sembly. We attended the assembly in order to study the behavior of the Khamba and other Tibetan emigrants who attended the assembly as pretended Tibetan representatives. But we did not recognize or sign the new constitutional law *(Shefa)* which was then made.

As for 1948, our mission in Nanking, namely the Khandon Losum, also attended the Chinese Assembly as visitors but no special representative was deputed from Lhasa, and they similarly did not recognize or sign the resolutions of the assembly.

21. In 1947 after India became independent, in reply to a communication from the Tibetan Government, the Government of India replied as follows:

"The Government of India would be glad to have an assurance that it is the intention of the Tibetan Government to continue relations on the existing basis until new agreements are reached on matters that either party may wish to take up. This is the procedure adopted by all other countries with which India has inherited treaty relations from His Majesty's Government."

22. Between 1912 and till the Seventeen-Point Agreement was signed on May 23, 1951, Tibet continued to conduct its foreign affairs without reference to any outside authority. Tibetan delegations in 1946 and in 1948 traveled extensively on Tibetan passports.

23. Mr. H. E. Richardson, who was in charge of the British and later Indian Mission at Lhasa, stated to the Legal Inquiry Committee on Tibet, constituted by the International Commission of Jurists that, . . . "the duties of the Officer in Charge of the British and later Indian Mission at Lhasa after 1936 were principally to conduct the diplomatic business of his Government with the Tibetan Government" (page 146 of the report entitled "Tibet and the Chinese Peoples Republic").

24. The foregoing facts should suffice to show that Tibet was completely independent. Since, however, doubts were raised last year regarding the status of my country, the following facts may be usefully stated:

25. Sir Eric Teichmann in *Affairs of China* wrote: "Since (1912) no vestige of Chinese authority has survived or reappeared in Lhasa-ruled Tibet. In more than twenty years he (the Thirteenth Dalai Lama) ruled as undisputed master of autonomous Tibet, preserving internal peace and order and maintaining close and intimate relations with the Indian Government."

26. In 1928 Sir Charles Bell in *The People of Tibet* pointed out that Chinese authority in Tibet had ceased.

27. M. Amaury de Riencourt who was in Tibet in 1947, states, "Tibet ruled itself in all respects as an independent nation." He goes on to say that "Government's writ ran everywhere."

28. Tsung Lien-shen and Shen Chi-liu who were both members of the Chinese Mission in Lhasa, say, "Since 1911 Lhasa has to all practical purposes enjoyed full independence." In support of this they mention that Tibet had its own currency and customs, its own telegraph and postal service, and its own civil service different from that of China, and its own army.

29. In 1950 when the proposal of El Salvador to place the question of the invasion of Tibet on the agenda of the General Assembly was being considered, the Jam Saheb of Nawanagar, the representative of India said his government had given careful study to the problems raised by the proposal of El Salvador to place the question of the invasion of Tibet by foreign forces on the General Assembly agenda. That was a matter of vital interest to both China and India. The Committee was aware that India, as a neighbor of both China and Tibet, with both of which it had friendly relations, was the country most interested in a settlement of the

problem. That was why the Indian government was particularly anxious that it should be settled peacefully. (A/BUR/SR. 73, page 19)

30. The claim of the Chinese to suzerainty over Tibet is based on the 1907 Convention between Great Britain and Russia. It may be pointed out that Tibet was not a party to that Convention and was in no way bound by that Convention.

31. As the head of the Tibetan government I say that what happened on October 7, 1950, was a flagrant act of aggression on the part of China against my country.

32. The Tibetan government appealed to the United Nations for help. As a result of the defeat of the Tibetan army, and after the efforts of the Tibetan government to get the help of the United Nations had failed, we were compelled to send a delegation to Peking. The delegation was compelled to sign what is known as the Seventeen-Point Agreement on May 23, 1951.

33. The events since then and till my departure from Tibet in March, 1959, are too well known to require any detailed recounting. Even now refugees are coming into Nepal, Bhutan, Sikkim, and India practically every day. The number of the refugees is 43,500. From the accounts of these refugees, the oppression and wholesale terror, to which I referred in my letter to you last year and also this year, have in no way lessened.

34. In this connection may I draw the attention of the United Nations to the excellent reports on the question of Tibet published by the International Commission of Jurists. In the second report, the distinguished Committee that closely examined the question came to the conclusion, *inter alia,* that Chinese authorities had been guilty of genocide within the meaning of the Genocide Convention. I trust that the United Nations will carefully examine the facts on which this conclusion is based and will take appropriate action to

deal with this matter. Genocide, even apart from the Genocide Convention, has been recognized as a crime against International Law.

35. As a result of a wholesale breach of all the important terms of the Seventeen-Point Agreement, the General Assembly (consisting of officials and public, mainly the public) repudiated that Agreement, as it was well entitled to do, and reasserted the independence of Tibet on March 10, 1959.

36. The fighting in Tibet against the occupiers and the oppressors is still going on. I appealed to the United Nations last year, and I am making this appeal again in the hope that the United Nations will take appropriate measures to get China to vacate its aggression. In my opinion, any measure short of this is not going to be of much help to my country where the Communist steamroller is every day crushing out the freedom of my people.

37. May I request Your Excellency to place this Appeal before the United Nations.

The Dalai Lama

The General Assembly

Recalling the principles regarding fundamental human rights and freedoms set out in the Charter of the United Nations and in the Universal Declaration of Human Rights adopted by the General Assembly on 10 December 1948,

Considering that the fundamental human rights and freedoms to which the Tibetan people, like all others, are entitled include the right to civil and religious liberty for all without distinction,

Mindful also of the distinctive cultural and religious heritage of the people of Tibet and of the autonomy which they have traditionally enjoyed,

Gravely concerned at reports, including the official statements of His Holiness the Dalai Lama, to the effect that the fundamental rights and freedoms of the people of Tibet have been forcibly denied them,

Deploring the effect of these events in increasing international tension and in embittering the relations between peoples at a time when earnest and positive efforts are being made by responsible leaders to reduce tension and improve international relations,

1. *Affirms its belief* that respect for the principles of the Charter of the United Nations and of the Universal Declaration of Human Rights is essential for the evolution of a peaceful world order based on the rule of law;

2. *Calls* for respect for the fundamental human rights of the Tibetan people and for their distinctive cultural and religious life.

834th plenary meeting,
21 October 1959

QUESTION OF TIBET

Resolution of the General Assembly—Sixteenth Session (1961)

Recalling its resolution 1353 (XIV) of 21 October 1959 on the question of Tibet,

Gravely concerned at the continuation of events in Tibet including the violation of fundamental human rights of the Tibetan people, suppression of their distinctive cultural and religious life which they have traditionally enjoyed,

Noting with deep anxiety the severe hardships which these events have inflicted on the Tibetan people as evidenced by the large scale exodus of Tibetan refugees to the neighboring countries,

Considering that these events violate fundamental human rights and freedoms set out in the Charter of the United Nations and the Universal Declaration of Human Rights, including the principle of self-determination of peoples and nations, and have the deplorable effect of increasing international tension and embittering relations between peoples,

1. *Reaffirms its conviction* that respect for the principles of the Charter and of the Universal Declaration of Human Rights is essential for the evolution of a peaceful world order based on the rule of law:

2. *Solemnly renews* its call for the cessation of practices which deprive the Tibetan people of their fundamental human rights and freedoms including their right to self-determination:

3. *Expresses the hope that* member States will make all possible efforts toward achieving the purposes of the present resolution.

Index

His Holiness the Dalai Lama

Born on July 6, 1935, in Taktser, northeastern Tibet, Tenzin Gyatso was recognized at the age of two as the fourteenth Dalai Lama, the spiritual and temporal leader of Tibet. In 1949, when China invaded Tibet, full temporal authority over the country was formally given to the Dalai Lama at age sixteen.

In March 10, 1959, when a popular uprising was brutally suppressed by Chinese forces, the Dalai Lama fled into exile to India with 80,000 Tibetans. A government-in-exile was established, with a democratically elected Parliament with the twin objective of taking care of the Tibetan refugees and to provide a base for the struggle to regain Tibet.

In 1987, the Dalai Lama announced a Five-Point Peace Plan for Tibet. The plan proposed a negotiated solution to the Tibetan problem, which took into consideration the interests of both Tibetans and Chinese. Since 1983, the Dalai Lama has publicly expressed his desire to at least visit Tibet, and in 1991 he called upon the world community to assist him.

In recognition of his efforts and achievement, the Dalai Lama has been conferred numerous awards and honorary doctorate degrees. In 1989 he was awarded the Nobel Peace Prize.

The Dalai Lama continues his efforts to this day to open a dialogue with the Chinese leadership and bring a peacefully negotiated settlement to Tibet.

For more information on Tibet contact:

International Campaign for Tibet
1825 K Street, suite 520
Washington, D.C. 20006
Phone: 202-785-1515
email: ict@peacenet.org

The Office of Tibet
241 East 32nd Street
New York, New York 10016
Phone: 212-213-5010